THE MIND
POLLUTERS

THE MIND POLLUTERS

by

Jerry R. Kirk

THOMAS NELSON PUBLISHERS
Nashville • Camden • New York

Published in Nashville, Tennessee, by Thomas Nelson, Inc. and distributed in Canada by Lawson Falle, Ltd., Cambridge, Ontario.

Printed in the United States of America.

Scripture quotations are from the Revised Standard Version of the
Bible, copyrighted 1946, 1952, © 1971, 1973 by the Division of Chris-
tian Education of the National Council of Churches of Christ in the
U.S.A. and used by permission.

The excerpts from "The War Within: An Anatomy of Lust" in chapter
four are from *Leadership* magazine and are used by permission.

Library of Congress Cataloging in Publication Data
Kirk, Jerry R.
   The mind polluters.

   Bibliography: p. 219
   1. Pornography—Religious aspects—Christianity.
2. Pornography—United States. I. Title.
BV4597.6.K57   1985   241'.667   85-13762
ISBN 0-8407-5965-7

DEDICATED

To the children, young people, and adults who have been victims of "mind pollution";*

To Starr Luteri-Hicks, whose careful research and writing were foundational and essential to produce the final product;

To Sarah Blanken, Sharlyn Stare, Tom Grossmann, and Peter Gillquist whose help and encouragement made the book possible;

To the staff and members of College Hill Presbyterian Church whose love and partnership in ministry have set me free and led me to seek the righteousness of God with freedom and joy;

To the leaders of Citizens Concerned for Community Values and the National Coalition Against Pornography, warriors of the past and servant-leaders of the future, whose partnership in ministry has inspired me to believe God for righteousness in the church and a moral revolution in the nation;

Finally, to my family—Patty, my dear wife and lifelong companion; the Scott Hahn family; the Mark Harrington family; the Timothy Kirk family; Kristen and Stephen, whose well-being is worth fighting for and whose generation is worth dying for.

*The stories told in this book are true and represent real persons. However, names, places, and times have been changed in order to protect their anonymity and pain.

CONTENTS

PART I
Survey of the Damage

Chapter 1

A Time to Stand

If I straighten the pictures on the walls of your home, I am committing no sin, am I? But suppose that your house were afire, and I still went calmly about straightening pictures, what would you say? Would you think me merely stupid or very wicked?...The world today is on fire. What are you doing to extinguish the fire?
Corrie ten Boom, *Amazing Love*, 101

The walkway where I was standing, in front of Cincinnati City Hall, was crowded with people. Women in light coats chatted nervously, business men in three-piece suits glanced about self-consciously, elderly people wore grim and determined expressions.

A van pulled up to the curb and six or eight more people scrambled out, all from my congregation. I smiled and waved, and their faces brightened. "Hey, we're gonna do it!" someone called.

"You betcha! Victory!" I answered with the thumbs-up sign, and tried to look more confident than I felt. Over four hundred citizens had promised to come this afternoon, and it looked as if that many were there and more. City council would have to hear us now.

"Jerry, what are you doing here?"

A good friend stood at my shoulder, and his expression showed more concern than I wanted to see.

"I saw your letter in *The Enquirer*, and heard that you were leading this—this demonstration or whatever it is. I couldn't believe it. This isn't like you, Jerry. Why are you doing this?"

"Bob, the situation is critical. If we don't make a stand now, there will be no stopping it. Somebody has to speak out before it's too late."

"But, Jerry, why you? You've got so much at stake—your church, your family, your reputation in the denomination. Why risk all of that? Is it publicity you want? Is it attention in the national news? You're going to get it, you know. Or is it political? Is that what you're after?"

There wasn't time to answer. The door to the council chambers opened, and people began to file in. But his questions stuck in my mind. And though I couldn't answer him, I found that I had to face his question and find the answer myself. What *was* I after?

THE LAST THING I NEED

I have absolutely no desire to go out and fight for causes. My goal as a pastor is to equip our laypersons well enough that when a good cause comes along, they will address it themselves! From the time I came to know Jesus Christ as my Savior and Lord thirty-five years ago, my joy has come through introducing men and women and young people to Him, and then nurturing and equipping them to go out and minister to others. I have never felt any "emotional need" to look for causes.

The only battle I've felt compelled to fight has been

the battle of time, to find enough hours in the day to talk to all the people, to study deeply enough in the Scriptures, to linger long enough in prayer, to meet with all the committees...and then to get home and play some tennis with my kids. The last thing I need is another crusade to take me away from my family and my church.

But something was happening, and reluctantly, with hands clenched and heels dug into the ground, I couldn't ignore it any longer. Something was happening to my community, to my congregation, to our young people.

It wasn't until a group of people in our congregation came and asked me to study and teach on the sexual revolution and immorality in America that I began to open my eyes. Still, I refused at first because I didn't have the time to study any "new issue," and I really didn't believe that this was a priority for a busy, overscheduled pastor. This so-called new sexual freedom was just the constant, inevitable sinful condition of fallen humanity, no better or worse than it had been from ages past, I thought.

But gradually, month by month, individuals kept coming to me with broken hearts and broken lives, asking for counsel, asking for help.

"Could you pray with me for my sister? She called me last night, and said that her husband walked out on her and the children. They've been married twelve years last November."

"Can I talk with you? I'm concerned for my kids at the junior high. An instructor was reprimanded last week for improper conduct toward a student. Supposedly he bit a seventh-grader on the bottom. No, I don't mean he spanked her. He bit her. I talked to several of the other teachers and they didn't seem all that offended. In fact, several of the men teachers thought it was very funny."

"Jerry, I need to talk with you, please, right now. My son has been arrested. They say he molested a little eight-year-old, and he's admitted that it's true. What should I do? Where did I go wrong?"

What's happening to our kids? What's happening to us?

Against my resistance, the realization grew that there was something more pervasive, something more evil than just a new frankness about sex. I began to realize that at some point, the moral behavior of the nation had shifted, and I had ignored the transition. But now my people were crying out for guidance and, while I knew the answer for any situation was God's grace and healing in Jesus Christ, I didn't understand the source of the problem. I found that I had no answer for the avalanche of immorality that was crushing my people. I wasn't sure where the real problem was.

THE NEW AMERICAN LIFESTYLE

Nearly half the marriages in the United States end in divorce. We've all heard that statistic. Most children have some kind of outside-the-home daycare before kindergarten because there is no adult who stays home to rear them. Single-parent families are accepted in the church and out of the church; kids go away in the summer to visit their dads and stepmothers, just like all their friends do. "Just Divorced" party balloons float beside those marked "Just Married" and "It's a Boy!" above the card racks in the malls. The new etiquette delicately allows for casual comments like, "his children," "my ex," while lawyers advertise new easy-term rates for divorce on television commercials.

It's the new American way of life. Only the stuffed shirts, prudes, and neo-puritans are shocked. "We're more honest about sex now," they say. "I do my own thing; I look out for myself." Society supposedly has a more healthy attitude toward sexuality than earlier generations, and the church ought to catch up with the times. But a never-ending line of hurting people marches through my office. In fact, it's growing longer every day, as more parents and wives and husbands try somehow to keep their families and their lives together.

What are the roots of this "new lifestyle"? When did we begin to turn away from the sanctity of the home, from the security of marriage, from modesty and chastity? When did those words become trite, humorous, old-fashioned? What happened to the innocence of youth, to blushing young brides, to heroes who were admired for faithfulness and self-control?

A mother asked me to talk with her young daughter. The girl had grown up in Sunday school, had attended a young people's confirmation class and her family was respected in the community. I knew the family well and respected them. A young teen-ager and pregnant.

"But everybody does it," she said, "and they made fun of me because I was, uh, you know.... "

"Because you were a virgin?"

"Yeah." She twisted a strand of streaked blond hair around her finger and ran her tongue across the braces in her little mouth. "Most of my friends have

15

done it with two or three boys, and they were saying that I was weird, you know, queer, because I hadn't. And I thought Jim would be nice, and it wouldn't be so bad, 'cause he goes to church, too, like me. And we used this stuff he got at the supermarket. But I guess we didn't use enough, or it didn't work, or something. So Mom's really mad at me."

No more had I finished talking with this young person than the phone rang.

"Jerry, I'm sorry to call you so late, but I wanted to let you know before it comes out in the papers in the morning. Carl Emerson was picked up tonight in a park near the university for indecent exposure. He's out on bail, but there's going to be a big stink." Carl Emerson is a widely known physician in town and a leader with area Boy Scouts.

WHERE ARE THE HEROES NOW?

In the secure circle of Christian friends and activities with which I'd been so busy, I had missed what was really going on. Maybe a lot of us in the evangelical community, with all of our striving to serve the Lord and His people, had just overlooked these crucial changes in society. Of course, it's important to keep ourselves separated from sin. Yes, we need to know our weaknesses and avoid temptation. But have we separated ourselves so far from "the world" that we no longer see what is happening there, and to people we love?

From the sewer of human suffering that flowed through my office door, it was evident that my people and their children were under moral attack. One morning, before dawn, early in the spring of 1982, I walked up onto a hillside across the street from my home. I reached out in my heart to God. What is happening, Lord? What is causing this flood of filth and immorality and destruction among Your people?

The answer, or at least a large part of the answer, had been all around me, but I hadn't seen it. I didn't want to see it. But the young people were seeing it. The adults in the community were seeing it, and it was growing more and more powerful and pervasive every week.

I didn't want to look at the new levels of sexual candor in the cinema. I didn't want to look at the magazines that were filling the newsstands. I didn't want to hear the rock music the kids were listening to, day and night. I didn't want to know what was coming into people's living rooms via videos and cable television and I didn't spend enough time watching commercial TV to realize the change taking place there.

I wanted to keep those images out of my head, to keep my thoughts on the things of God, on a level of beauty and innocence and purity. I thought that a leader of God's people didn't need to know all that junk—in fact, *ought* not to know those things.

For the first time, as the night slowly turned into gray morning mist, I felt ready to face the source of the immorality that was shattering people's marriages and slaughtering our young people. It seemed, as I stood on that hillside at daybreak, praying over the immorality of our country and the direction we were heading in the church, that I was watching the *Titanic* steaming through the fog toward the iceberg with no one to guide her.

We are steaming full speed ahead toward certain moral destruction. Why doesn't somebody, anybody, go for the bridge and change course?

Chapter 2

The Death of Righteousness

I demand righteousness and a right relationship with you.
I demand justice and a compassionate integrity toward all.
I demand that you stick by My standards and insist that
you do the right thing toward others for the right reasons.
The picture of Me that you make in your own mind so that
you feel complacent and secure is idolatry. You think jus-
tice blind, but My justice is open-eyed; it passionately
seeks out wrong and tries to right it. It is dedicated to
other people's needs, and especially the needs of those less
able to care for themselves.

William Bontrager's paraphrase of Amos in
Charles Colson's *Loving God,* 157

Remember the pinups—lots of beautiful legs, Betty
Grable and Dorothy Lamour in halters or two-piece
bathing suits? The gas station man in town usually
let the kids hang around his garage, where they could
catch a glimpse of the girlie calendars, often with pictures of girls partially or totally nude from the waist
up. *Esquire* had a centerfold—generously endowed, to
be sure, but always vested in swimwear.

Then there was the stack of *National Geographics*
beneath the basement stairs. Mom thought we were
looking up maps for geography class. But instead, we
were busily searching through those musty pages for

that article on European Neanderthals, with artists'
illustrations of half-naked prehistoric women, in their
aprons of skins and necklaces of saber-tooth tiger's
claws. Heavy-duty stuff, for sure!

Movies

It wasn't all that long ago that Ingrid Bergman's
movies were banned from the United States because
in real life she gave birth to illegitimate children. Or
that "Gone with the Wind" barely squeaked past the
review boards when Rhett Butler dared to say,
"Frankly, my dear, I don't give a damn."

But then the movies began to change. Only the edited version of "From Here to Eternity" made it
through our community in 1953, but evidently Burt
Lancaster and Donna Reed had done something other
than look for sand dollars out on the beach that
night. In the midfifties, college fraternity groups
could rent "blue movies," showing what one today
might call modest nudity. "Vixen" was prosecuted in
Cincinnati, but the publicity probably added to its appeal in other parts of the country. As recently as
1968, "I am Curious, Yellow," and virtually all of the
"stag" movies were imported from Denmark and
Sweden.

Magazines

In the early fifties came the "skin" magazines,
Playboy being the first to be widely read, opening the
door to numerous others. Detailed depictions of genitalia began to appear in sleazy "men's magazines" in
1967 and 1968; then implied or "simulated" sexual
activity in June 1970. When *Penthouse* became the
first "slick" magazine to show a model's pubic hair in

April 1970, *Playboy* publisher Hugh Hefner was quoted as being offended: "That's not photography—that's pornography." But two years later, January 1972, *Playboy* printed the same kind of shots.

Depictions of bondage, spanking, and domination (women in leather or rubber clothes, with other accessories) were available in specialty magazines in limited quantities through the early seventies, usually in the large cities.[1] Now, in the mid-eighties, magazines showing all of these deviations and others are not available just under the counter, but are openly displayed on most magazine racks throughout the country.

Broadcasting

In 1960, the Kingston Trio scorched the radio waves with the lyrics: "I don't give a damn about the greenback dollar." In "Roots," 1976, bare-breasted, black African village women were shown on prime-time TV. "But it's historic, a valid representation of their culture," we said, and so it was. Then Archie Bunker changed his grandson's diapers while all America looked on. Frontal male nudity! But he's just a baby, for Pete's sake. Surely that's nothing to be upset about.

DOWN THROUGH THE RABBIT'S HOLE

When Hugh Hefner published his first issue of *Playboy* in 1953, Americans were gradually won over by his "good taste" and "high quality." The photos were beautifully done. Sure, there was lots of skin, but it was such *pretty* skin, and the girls were as refreshingly innocent as the girl next door, not brazen and cheap like the pulp pornography. This was high-class stuff.

And the articles were first-rate—interviews with presidents, physicians, and secular prophets, which helped set a standard for print journalism for the next twenty years.[2]

Hugh Hefner was a graduate of the University of Illinois, and knew how to market his product to collegiate America. Subscriptions were solicited from almost every fraternity house in the nation, and the *Playboy* centerfold suddenly became standard wallcovering in countless college fraternity and dorm rooms.

In his twenty-fifth anniversary issue, Hugh Hefner clearly stated the *Playboy* philosophy:

> We had intended *Playboy* to be a response to the repressive antisexual, anti-play-and-pleasure aspects of our puritan heritage....The *Playboy* philosophy is predicated on our belief in the importance of the individual and his rights as a member of a free society. That's our most basic premise....

The bulk of the article is not so much a statement of a philosophy as it is a compilation of charges against a caricature of American religion, as in the following:

> We would point out the utter lack of justification in the state's making unlawful certain private acts performed by two consenting adults. Organized religions may preach against them if they wish...but there can be no possible justification for religion's using the state to coercively control the sexual conduct of the members of a free society.[3]

The Mind Polluters

The articles and interviews in *Playboy* are still first-class. And the models are posed artistically, with an air of health and happiness...so natural, sipping a mug of milk. "Wholesomeness" is expressed in choice of colors and setting and by photography techniques that present soft, romantic images. The viewer gets the impression that this is really a nice girl. Her blouse slipped a little, but she's a sweet kid. But you see, it's this very clean and wonderful appearance that is so insidious.

Everybody recognizes ugly evil as evil, but pretty, innocent-looking evil? It was a marketing technique, and it worked. America bought pornography when it was wrapped in beautiful, healthy packaging.

The twenty-five year progression didn't stop at the bunny's door. Hugh Hefner's wholesome-appearing bunny opened the way for America to fall through the rabbit hole into a wonderland of perversion: *Penthouse, Hustler, Oui*, and all the rest. In this looking-glass world of human flesh, everything is reversed: goodness is bad, naughtiness is nice, and darkness is light. Milton had a line, "Evil, be thou my good"!

The distortion spreads from the sex magazines to journalism in general. *Cosmopolitan, Glamour, Redbook*, and other women's magazines present increasingly provocative covers and/or articles promoting promiscuity, selling the message that "women really want it this way." *Vogue* magazine, December 1975, had a fashion feature with a couple modeling jump-suits, where the male model is violently slapping the female model. *Sports Illustrated's* annual swimsuit edition has a not-very-subtle message: sex is sport, specifically, a man's sport, and women are free game. Here we are again. The woman is less than human, the freely mating rabbit, the object of the hunter.

Very few mature Christians have explored the bunny's territory, and with sound reasons. Some of those who have ventured this way have lost themselves in the moral confusion that champions the "courage" of sophisticated immorality.

WARNING: ENEMY TERRITORY

We must enter this area with a battlefield mentality. The struggle against pornography is not only difficult but dangerous, and anybody who approaches obscenity must be equipped like a soldier approaching a battlefield. We must identify the enemy, our methods of fighting, and our resources for offense and defense. In every battle, it's deadly to go wandering around in enemy territory unarmed and unprepared.

Several years ago, the mayor of a major southern city was concerned about the quality of motion pictures coming through the community. He appointed a task force of five widely known, highly respected professional persons to view the "adult" films and make recommendations as far as content and quality. Within one year, four of the five members of the task force had themselves become involved in adultery and scandal. Doubly disappointing, all were professing followers of Jesus Christ. It would seem apparent that constant exposure to pornographic material, even with the purest intentions, is dangerous.

The Book of Proverbs has some words of wisdom for any of us who would approach the *Playboy* bunny and her associates:

Do not desire her beauty in your heart,
and do not let her capture you with her eyelashes;
for a harlot may be hired for a loaf of bread,
but an adulteress stalks a man's very life....
for many a victim has she laid low; yea, all her slain
are a mighty host.
Her house is the way to Sheol,
going down to the chambers of death (Prov. 6:25-26;
7:26-27).

Notice this doesn't say the victim will lose his virginity, but his life. We are talking about something that cannot only affect the body, but also deaden the soul. For Solomon warns, "He does not know that it will cost him his life" (Prov. 7:23).

Maybe you are one who, like myself, has not looked to see what the magazines or movies or peep shows are really like. Or maybe you have seen them five or ten or twenty years ago, but have kept away from them since. If that's the case, you need to know exactly what you're up against.

DESCENT INTO HELL

I had a layover in Chicago's O'Hare airport not long ago, and decided to stroll through the newsstand area and find out exactly what was being displayed and sold. I spent about an hour perusing the range of magazines, starting with *Playboy*, which is the least offensive of the porn sheets, then *High Society, Chic, Hustler*, and all the rest.

I actually became physically ill. The magazines not only display total nudity with focus on the genitals, they are promoting and displaying sexual intercourse with penetration; homosexual intercourse; oral, anal, and group sex. Bestiality—copulation with animals—is right there in living color: men with pigs, women with dogs or horses. And specialty publications cater to every imaginable perversion, from foot fetishists to sadists to transvestites.

In a study by P.E. Dietz and Barbara Evans, published in the November 1982 issue of the *American Journal of Psychiatry*, it was reported that the change in the pornographic market over the past decade has not been widely recognized. Materials in the late sixties and early seventies when many major studies were done, were almost entirely limited to nude women posed alone, but now that category represents only 10 percent of the market.

Nearly 90 percent of the "adults only" publications major in images that were strictly "under the counter" in the seventies. Vaginal and oral intercourse, spanking, enema administration, pregnancy, anal intercourse, and especially transvestite images are now among the most popular.

This study included only the illustrations on the *covers* of the magazines. The report indicates that "the prevalence of a specific type of imagery in pornography is an unobtrusive measure of the prevalence of the corresponding fantasy among the consumers."[4] In other words, the pictures on the magazines reflect exactly what is going on in the customer's imagination.

We hear the terms *soft* and *hard-core* pornography, but the distinction is hazy. Soft porn usually refers to a magazine like *Playboy*, where most of the photos are simple nudity, without perversion or depictions of explicit sexual activity. But in soft porn, anything up to actual penetration and ejaculation can be pictured.

The Mind Polluters

The new erotic paperback novel or romance series from Dell (Amber), Bantam (Anonymous), and Playboy (Christina) are classified as soft porn, and are well accepted on the general market. The two big bookstore chains, B. Dalton and Waldenbooks, are openly accepting these paperbacks.

Hard-core usually includes materials that show penetration, ejaculation, or explicit sexual violence like rape, mutilation, and "S and M" or sadomasochism, the modern code word for the sadistic inflicting of pain by one sex partner on the other for sexual gratification. Another category is Nazi porn, depicting sexual torture and rape with the holocaust as background.[5]

This takes us right into the scum of the matter. Sadomasochism is brutality, plain and simple. It expresses the mentality that persons can enjoy being bound and beaten as an expression of sexuality; that women actually enjoy—even crave—being raped; that violence in sex can be fun for both parties. Interestingly, Dietz and Evans avoid labeling any portion of the materials in their study "sadomasochistic," because they find that "sadism and masochism, in the broadest sense, play a part in all pornography."

None of these expressions are limited to printed material, of course. Movies and videos have opened up a whole new realm to pornographers. Not limited to still photos of sex, one can now watch sex in action right in his own den or living room. Oral and anal penetration, bestiality (also called zoophilism), and mutilation are common and available. There is a new genre called "slasher" films in which the "hero" does just that—slashes the victim before or after raping her. Murdering the woman and raping the dead body is another variation technically called necrophilia, sex with the dead.

The Dietz and Evans report states, "Some photographs are such that it would take little suspension of disbelief to imagine that the woman was dead ...[shopkeepers] complained that [pictures showing blood] 'sell out so fast we can't keep them in stock.' "[6] All of this is right down the road at the drive-in theater and the "adult" book shop, and soon will be coming into the living room on cable television unless the American public steps forward with a firm and resolute "No."

Then there are snuff films—films of actual murders. Two men in Orange County, California, have been charged with murdering two teen-age girls, apparently photographing the crime.[7] Rumors tell of the production and circulation in underground smut rings of snuff films that are far more explicit than the staged violence of "legal" films.

Most frightening of all is child pornography, "kiddie porn." What would you do if you saw a man raping a little child? Would you be enraged? Would you rush to stop it? Hundreds and thousands of young children, boys and girls, are being raped in front of cameras in the United States today, and their rapists are getting rich. Officials estimated in 1983 as many as three hundred thousand children and probably many more, from sixteen to less than six months old, are filmed or photographed while being raped, either for the molester's own gratification or for commercial purposes.[8]

The magazines are called *Lolli-Tots, Baby Sex, Lolita Love*, and there are many more. Little boys are just as vulnerable as little girls; *Chicken Supreme* is a publication that specializes in sexual exploitation of young boys. Incest is a favorite theme; *Father and Daughter*, for example. F.B.I. supervisory special agent Ken Lanning reports that many of the photos in these magazines are taken in the United States, of American children, and that the pictures are then sold to producers in Northern Europe for worldwide distribution in commercial child pornography magazines.[9]

A sex manual for molesters, *How to Have Sex With Kids*, is available through mail-order distributors and has turned up in bookstores across the country. Reportedly produced by individuals associated with the Austin Pedophile Study Group II, in Austin, Texas, the booklet explains how to meet children; how to persuade them to have anal, oral, vaginal, masturbatory, and group sex; and how to keep these activities secret from the children's parents.[10]

At least two national organizations actively promote sexual use of children: the René Guyon Society whose motto is "Sex before eight or it's too late"; and the North American Man/Boy Love Association (N.A.M.B.L.A.), a homosexual group that advocates the abolition of all age-of-consent restrictions. These groups argue that modern families are so devoid of warm affectionate touching that sexual abuse is a healthy alternative for the children, and that pedophiles have just as much right to practice their sexual preference as any other "normal" person. According to the *Playboy* philosophy, why not?

Author Judianne Densen-Gerber wrote:

> Today's sexual revolution, which is perhaps better called the sexual holocaust, has radically altered the whole fabric of society....There seem to be almost no

parameters of conduct, no limitations on behavior. Permissiveness is exalted. Those of us from past generations have no anchors to secure us.

Our parents had firm ideas of right and wrong. When we misbehaved, we may have felt hypocritical and a bit guilty, but at least we had value systems against which we could test ourselves. Today, with sexual freedom leading more often to license than to happiness, our children have become frightened, alienated, and isolated. They search for intimacy in immediate genital gratification rather than in sustained caring relationships.[11]

LIBERTY AND LICENSE

In the United States, with all of our freedoms and rights, we often assume that if something exists, it is because it is protected under the law. Or we assume that it must be harmless because if it weren't, the government wouldn't allow it. So we turned our head when the movies went sour, and we walked down the other side of the street when the "adult" bookstore moved in, and we didn't do anything about it. We didn't think we could. But we were mistaken.

Pornography is not harmless. It is deadly. When the sex shop opens in the neighborhood, far more is at stake than the value of our real estate. Obscenity is not and never was protected by the First Amendment or any other section of the Constitution. Smut has no legal right to exist. The industry of immorality flourishes in America for one reason alone: the local community has not taken the steps to see that existing laws are enforced and that additional, more effective laws are written.

Let me say it again. *Obscenity has no legal right to exist.*

AVAILABILITY

We are not protected from the pollution of pornography simply because we may not have "adult" bookstores or X-rated theaters in our neighborhood. Sending our kids to Christian schools doesn't shelter them from immorality. We need to open our eyes and realize that, like air pollution and water pollution, moral pollution affects us all. Like it or not, unless we begin to take strong action, it's only going to get worse. The pornographers never know when to quit.

We hear about the publishers' rights to print and distribute what they please. But few people stand up for another equally important right, our right to refuse to be exposed to unlimited filth. When is enough, enough? When is enough too much? Anybody has the right to be naked in the bathroom. But nobody has the right to expose himself on the street corner. That is the issue we must stress.

You have the right to be protected from pornography—but that right is increasingly being denied. It used to be that the smut was downtown in the "red-light district," and nice people just didn't go there. Then it was just at "those" theaters; in "that" part of town; in the massage parlors; or, at least, under the counter. No longer. It's on nearly every newsstand, it's in the drugstore, it's in the gas station and convenience store. In many places, every form of indecency is displayed openly, in full view and reach of minors, and seldom are the publications wrapped in cellophane to prevent casual browsing. Catalogs pandering everything from leather jock straps to inflatable sex partners come unsolicited through the mail.

Commercial television is pushing propriety to the limit in every area and intentionally extending its moral boundaries with each new season. The soaps, it seems, pave the way for television license, as hospital rooms and divorce courts give way to explicit bedroom scenes. Prime-time is experimenting in the furthest extremes of violence and vocabulary, and TV comedy is slipping more and more toward the night-club entertainment style of George Carlin and Richard Pryor.

But the frontline in pornography is now the cable television networks and the videotape industry where the F.C.C. and existing broadcasting regulations presently have no authority. As the Rev. Morton Hill of Morality in Media has said, "Pornography is no longer downtown—it's downstairs."

Playboy Channel, and its competitor, Pleasure Channel, both offer sexually explicit films. Other local public access cable channels commonly feature nudity. In 1984, over 40 percent of all TV households in the United States had access to cable, with 90 percent expected to have access in 1990. The Playboy Channel alone boasted 650,000 subscribers in 1984. Channel "J" in New York City features a talkshow in which the naked cohosts fondle one another in front of the camera, with commercial breaks where sponsors advertise "escort services" for one hour or the entire night. Prostitution is for sale over cable TV.

Although the National Cable Television Association recommends that members refrain from transmitting X-rated films, many of the "adult" services include "hard-R's"—hard-core films with close-ups of penetration edited out. The cable services claim exemption from broadcasting pornography regulations because they are transmitted through wire rather than the airwaves.

They further justify the content of their programs on the theory that cable services only come directly into the homes of subscribers and that "lock-boxes" are provided to ensure protection for minors. Reports indicate, however, that numbers of people are witnessing cable porn channels filtering through other stations, and loud and clear audio portions of sexual activity can be heard. Because of this, cable pornography is literally forced into the homes of citizens who want no part of it.

Forty million homes are now equipped with videotape recorders, and the popularity of obscene videotapes has skyrocketed. The market for X-rated videotapes in the Los Angeles area alone was estimated at two hundred million dollars in 1982 and growing fast. According to Arthur Morowitz, the president of New York's Video Shack chain, "When people buy their tape deck, they buy a kiddie movie for their child and an X-rated movie for themselves. It's the standard starter kit."[12]

In the spring of 1984, police near Atlanta seized eight hundred X-rated videocassettes from a warehouse and two hundred more from a home in Dekalb County. Texas state legislator Doyle Willis has said, "One of the things we are worried about in home video is people getting children and making their own films. This has increased tremendously in the last year."[13]

Who publishes and distributes the masses of pulp magazines and fills the warehouses full of films and videos? Who is pushing the smut onto cable television in spite of community protests? How do the pornographers persist in spite of repeated convictions and Supreme Court rulings against them?

ENDNOTES

1. Joseph L. Galloway and Jeanne Thornton, "Crackdown on Pornography–A No-Win Battle," *U.S.News and World Report*, June 4, 1984, 84.

2. How does *Playboy* attract and maintain such quality? According to the 1981 *Writer's Market*, a four- to six-thousand-word article pays two thousand dollars minimum; an interview, three thousand dollars; short story, two thousand dollars. All are paid on acceptance with generous "kill-fee" if the piece is not actually used. By comparison, *Popular Mechanics* pays three to six hundred dollars for two-thousand-word articles; *Christianity Today*, one hundred dollars, minimum.

3. The article in the twenty-fifth anniversary issue is actually a collection of excerpts from the original *"Playboy* Philosophy" series which ran in twenty-five installments beginning in December 1962.

4. Park Elliott Dietz and Barbara Evans, "Pornographic Imagery and Prevalence of Paraphilia," *American Journal of Psychiatry*, 139:11, Nov. 1982, 1493.

5. Aric Press and others, "The War Against Pornography," *Newsweek*, March 18, 1985, 61.

6. Dietz and Evans.

7. *U.S. News and World Report*, June 4, 1984, 84.

8. Rita Rooney, "Innocence For Sale," *Ladies' Home Journal*, April 1983, 79.

9. Kenneth Lanning, supervisory special agent, Behavioral Science Unit, F.B.I. Academy, testifying before the Hearing Concerning Sexually Explicit Publications, U.S. Senate Subcommittee on Juvenile Justice, August 8, 1984.

10. Claire Dawson-Brown, assistant county attorney, Travis County, Texas, testifying before the Hearing Concerning Sexually Explicit Publications, U.S. Senate Subcommittee on Juvenile Justice, August 8, 1984.

11. Sam Janus, *The Death of Innocence* (New York: William Morrow, 1981), 10.

12. Press, "The War Against Pornography," 61.

13. Galloway, "Crackdown on Pornography—A No-Win Situation," 84.

Chapter 3

How Big Is the Problem?

For the wrath of God is revealed from heaven against all ungodliness and wickedness of men who by their wickedness suppress the truth....For this reason God gave them up to dishonorable passions. Their women exchanged natural relations for unnatural, and the men likewise gave up natural relations with women and were consumed with passion for one another, men committing shameless acts with men and receiving in their own persons the due penalty for their error. And since they did not see fit to acknowledge God, God gave them up to a base mind and to improper conduct. They were filled with all manner of wickedness, evil, covetousness, malice....Though they know God's decree that those who do such things deserve to die, they not only do them but approve those who practice them (Rom. 1:18, 26, 32).

"There are 20,000 adult bookstores, 400 adult magazines, more pornographic books and publishers than can be counted, and 800 adult movie houses, as well as mail-order firms and cable-television services that deal in pornographic matter. Some 400,000 pornographic videocassettes have been sold, and even pornographic videogames are on the market. More than 2 1/2 million people view pornographic movies each week...."[1]

Pornography stores in the United States outnumber McDonald's hamburger restaurants.

Dial-a-porn averages two-hundred thousand calls per month. Operating since 1982, one business maintains ninety answering machines. In 1983, as a carrier of the dial-a-porn message, the New York Telephone Co. was making twenty-five thousand dollars a day; the suppliers of the "service" made ten thousand dollars daily.[2]

Several lines of pornographic greeting cards are now available in certain gift and card shops. The "Rock Shots" line features transvestites, male genitals, and homosexual acts. "Exposed Cards—Screamers" specialize in sadism.

Comments John Court, "The person of Jesus himself is desecrated by obscenity and blasphemy with the purpose of ridiculing Christian beliefs."[3]

When I think about the context and pervasive presence of pornography in this society, it is overwhelming. Sometimes I wonder why in the world I'm trying to tackle a situation like this. Do you know that the F.B.I. has documented that 90 percent of the industry is run by organized crime?

There are only about a dozen major producers of pornographic materials—and most of these are the families that run the syndicate. It is a major industry, but it is concentrated; it is stoppable.

Back in 1978, *Forbes* magazine estimated that pornographers took in $16,438,000 a day. Estimates of recent gross sales run at least six billion dollars a year, and for 1985, we're hearing seven or eight billion. And, by the way, much of that is tax-free. A major portion of the profits are reinvested in the production of more such poison to continually lower the quality and standards of our lives.

DEEP THROAT

William Kelly was a special agent with the F.B.I. from 1952 until his retirement in 1980. He investigated the federal crime of interstate transportation of obscene matter and worked on cases of sexual exploitation of children. Bill Kelly has been employed since 1981 as consultant and special investigator of obscenity matters for the organized crime division of Broward County Sheriff's Office, Fort Lauderdale, and is a volunteer advisor to the Organized Crime Strike Force of the U.S. Department of Justice at Miami. He is also instructor on obscenity matters to police recruits and he lectures on obscenity and pornography to prosecutors, vice officers, and the public.

While working with us at the two National Consultations on Pornography in Cincinnati, Bill described some of his personal confrontations with organized crime and the extent of the Mafia involvement in pornography.

"A lot of these people are Mafia members, and I've known them one-on-one for many years. There are only about two hundred people in this country that are really important in the porno industry, and most all of them are involved in organized criminal activities across state lines—a violation of federal and state obscenity laws which are not being enforced.

"The MIPORN series of cases with national roundup of obscenity figures was the last great F.B.I. effort in traditional obscenity enforcement. The only thing they do today, and the only thing anybody does in the federal government, is the enforcement of the child obscenity laws. I'm telling you that from first-hand personal experience."

The MIPORN series was a "sting" operation that Bill participated in while working with the F.B.I. in Miami. Posing as distributors, two undercover F.B.I. agents were able to collect first-hand knowledge and evidence that led to a series of convictions, and which firmly established the connection of pornography with organized crime.

Because of the attention given by the media, many people are familiar with the names and even the personalities in some pornographic films. But very few realize the criminal powers behind these productions. Bill Kelly explains, "The movie 'Deep Throat' was produced in 1972, in Miami and New York City, for twenty-five thousand dollars. As of 1982, it had grossed just over fifty *million* dollars, which makes 'Deep Throat' by far the most productive motion picture film ever made in Miami, Florida. And they're still making money off it, because it's still in circulation."

"Deep Throat," starring Linda Lovelace, was the first of what are now called "porno chic" films and is considered a classic; it was fifty-nine minutes of mostly oral copulation. The producers were the Peraino element within the Colombo family of the Mafia. "It was produced, distributed, and enforced internationally (as was the film 'The Devil in Miss Jones'). The term *enforced* means that about 50 percent of the price of each ticket sold goes to the producers."

About 1973, the man who actually controlled "Deep Throat," Tony Peraino, informed an F.B.I. agent in Miami that if Bill Kelly would leave the "Deep Throat" case alone for two years, Peraino would be beyond the U.S. government's reach because of the riches he would have made from that film. He did, in fact, become rich; he was also convicted and sentenced. But even though the principals were convicted twice in Memphis federal court, they received only minor prison terms and fines.

"Now, what did the Peraino family do with the money from that movie?" asks Bill Kelly. "With the profits from 'Deep Throat,' the Perainos developed their own legitimate motion-picture film studio and distributed 'The Texas Chain-saw Massacre,' Andy Warhol's 'Frankenstein,' and 'The Return of the Dragon.' "

Yet we can still win against the porn producers. Even with the wealth and power of the syndicate behind them, other members of the Peraino clan were later convicted in U.S. District Court, Miami, and the subsequent sentencing was much heavier.

CHEAP PEEP

In addition to motion pictures shown in adult movie theaters, low quality "peep-show" films are produced to be marketed through the projection machines located in adult bookstores throughout the country. These are often the worst of the hard-core product, involving every imaginable sexual deviance. The peep-show booths are essentially private chambers where the customer often masturbates while viewing the film. One large midwestern firm reported taking six thousand dollars per day from the peep-show operations in one store.

"I'm being very conservative saying ten dollars a day per machine," Bill Kelly told us, "and that's only doing the film four times. It takes two dollars to two-fifty to see the film one time, at a quarter a shot. So if you only get four customers a day to see the whole film, there's your ten dollars. Now, if you've got twenty machines, which would be a good average per store, and the retailer makes ten dollars per day, which is awfully conservative, multiply that by the four-hundred thousand machines we know are out there, and you're up in the big money. That's 20 percent of your pornography market right there."

Kelly concludes, "You have to convince the country that dealing in obscenity is a civil crime as well as a moral crime. [Federal laws on the books right now make obscenity a civil crime.] It is the unfulfilled job of the Justice Department to see that those people are prosecuted. Otherwise, your efforts are in vain on a national level."

JOURNALISM JUNK

There are enough pornographic magazines printed each year to pave, covers alone, a two-lane highway from San Francisco to Washington, D.C. *Playboy* produces four million copies per month. *Penthouse* sells four thousand per hour, twenty-four hours a day, 365 days a year. Magazines alone produce about half a billion dollars per year for the porn syndicate.

In past years, "skin magazines" were available only by private subscription or from the sleazy stores in the bad part of town. But in recent years, pornography has made a major move into the suburbs.

As of March 1985, 7-Eleven is the leading retailer of pornographic magazines, such as *Playboy* and *Penthouse*, in America. Members of their own marketing department have told Dallas *Times Herald* columnist

John Bloom that they sell 20 percent of all *Playboy* magazines, and a similar percentage of *Penthouse.* 7-Eleven, which is a subsidiary of the Southland Corporation, interestingly refers to itself as a "family store" and supports such worthwhile projects as "Jerry's Kids" and the Olympics. They sell milk, eggs, bread, and pornography.

In apparent response to citizen complaints, 7-Eleven has removed some of the pornographic magazines from the shelves and put the remaining ones behind the counter. I commend them for that and for their support of the U.S. Olympic team, and for funding medical research. But the fact remains: pornographic magazines promote promiscuous use of drugs and a darkened sexual lifestyle that destroys family life, especially the lives of young people. And 7-Eleven remains the largest retailer of porn magazines in America.

According to Henry Boatwright, chairman of the U.S. Advisory Board for Social Concerns, 70 percent of the pornographic magazines sold in stores like 7-Eleven end up in the hands of minors. 7-Eleven cannot dodge the reality of that devastation—and its own moral responsibility—no matter how many good things it seeks to do as a company.

Over a period of years, several responsible individuals and organizations have met with 7-Eleven officials, urging them to stop selling the magazines. They have flatly refused, saying that their customers want the magazines and they want to serve their customers. Economics is the bottom line.

Other retailers, including the Consolidated Foods Corporation, the Dart Drug Corporation, Lil' Champ Food Stores, People's Drug, Revco, the Thrifty Corporation (as of spring 1985), have continued to sell "men's magazines." The decision by owners and managers of these stores to carry pornography has very little to do with morality. The issue is money.

Knowing that women find the skin magazines offensive, and that many of these family stores depend on women customers, pornographers have devised special incentives to persuade retailers to carry their publications. There is often an agreement between the manager and the distributor in which extra money is paid to the store to display smut on the front racks instead of behind the counter. Other bookstore owners claim that the local periodical distributors will not supply any magazines to their news racks unless the store will accept pornography in the package deal. One pornographic magazine costs twenty-five to fifty cents to produce and retails for three to twelve dollars.[4]

It's no wonder these people can afford to hire the top lawyers and experts to argue their cases through years of legal battles in the courts. Pornography is the third highest-profit industry in organized crime after narcotics and gambling, and the three areas are closely related.

Bruce Taylor is general counsel and vice-president of Citizens for Decency through Law, and formerly assistant prosecutor and assistant director of law for the city of Cleveland. He believes the true sales figure for pornography in general is grossly overestimated, and that we may be giving the porn industry more credit and credibility than it deserves. The enormous profit figures create the illusion that "everybody" must be buying the materials. When jurists see the figures, they sometimes leap to the conclusion that everybody wants it—making it socially acceptable, according to community standards.

In reality, says Taylor, not everybody is buying it. Certain repeat customers spend a large portion of their disposable income on pornography, and because of the enormous markup on a low-cost, low-quality product, the profit margin is very high.

In addition, Taylor strongly suspects that the seven-to-eight-billion-dollar-per-year figure includes at least two to four billion dollars in "laundered" cash from gambling, drug sales, and prostitution, funneled through the adult bookstores to avoid detection. "We know who the key figures are, and we know about the organized pornography syndicate because certain people have been convicted," says Taylor.

"One specific example is the Trambetas brothers who ran the Ellwest Stereo Theater out of Seattle, Washington. They were also running theaters in Jacksonville, Florida, and were indicted under the racketeering statute. They were closed down under a plea agreement, and made to promise not to operate or be involved in any obscenity operations in the state of Florida. Two years ago, Orlando closed down the five remaining bookstores and theaters they had under a racketeering case. So we know that: (1) organized crime is controlling most of the pornography industry; and (2) the effective way to shut them down is to utilize the state and federal racketeering statutes."

The federal Racketeer-Influenced and Corrupt Organizations law, known as R.I.C.O., covers a pattern of racketeering activity involving the felonies of murder, extortion, gambling, narcotics, bribery, robbery, and kidnapping. In October 1984, Congress passed the Helms Amendment which adds "dealing in obscenity" to federal R.I.C.O. It is now possible for federal law enforcement to effectively close down pornography operations and confiscate all property related to obscenity traffic. Therefore, we have a powerful new weapon to hit the pornographers in their profit, where it hurts most.

X-RATED LIVING ROOM

"Everything that's in these magazines is now being put onto cable TV. You see the woman removing her blouse, and the whole sex act, and it's a thousand times more arousing on TV than when you see it in print," comments Father Morton Hill, coauthor of the Hill-Link Minority Report of the 1970 Presidential Commission on Obscenity and Pornography. While working on the leadership team for the National Consultation, Father Hill stressed the urgency of confronting pornography on cable television.

"The cable people will insist that they don't show X-rated movies; they call it hard-R. All that means is that they take the X-rated films and edit out the close-up shots. That's what's on the *Playboy* Channel. And you can just imagine the warped image of women that is being portrayed on these channels every night.

"The material that I'm describing," explains Father Hill, "is getting to our children in their homes and in their friends' homes. I was watching a movie on the Showtime cable channel just a couple of months ago. I don't know if it was rated R or PG, but I suspect it was PG because it was directed toward the teens. The story was about this seventeen-year-old who flunked French, and a young woman came to tutor him for the summer. Pretty soon they're going all the way, and the whole thing is very arousing. That one film, viewed by a seventeen-year-old, could undo seventeen years of Christian training in a home.

"Or a young single woman, who may be dying for affection, may be prompted to believe it is very exciting to have intercourse with a teen-ager. And because she saw the film, she knows just how to go about it. And this one film was repeated about four or five times on Showtime, all at different times of the day, which means a tremendous audience. And that's just one film.

"We need to insist that the laws that are on the books now are vigorously enforced, especially at the federal level. And we must press for the passage of new cable regulations at the local and state levels. I'm talking about laws, not lock-boxes. A lock-box never stopped one of these ten-year-old electronic geniuses from getting what he wanted out of the TV. Children have been devising ways of getting the *Playboy* service by jiggling the cable connecters."

Father Hill makes a clear call to Christians. "Our goal has to be to decimate and destroy the illicit sex industry now, before it can complete its move into our homes by way of cable television. What we need is a velvet glove over a firm fist full of facts."[5]

SO WHAT?

Why should we care if people want to watch erotic programs on television in the privacy of their own homes?

We have already noted that cable porn channels have been known to bleed into other channels, interrupting other programs and bringing sexually explicit images or sound track into the homes of nonsubscribers. If anyone's rights are in danger, it is the right of decent persons to refuse to have obscenity imposed on them.

Other families have found that cable companies will not offer them services including family-centered movies, sports, or news channels unless they buy the whole package, including hard-rock music channels and/or sex channels.

But the far more important issue is that we have to live in the society influenced by cable television and video pornography. If our children don't watch cable porn or obscene videocassettes at home, they still live in the neighborhoods and go to school with children and young adults who do.

Just a few years ago, a mother and her little girl were watching "Born Innocent" on NBC, a program mild in comparison to films on the cable channels and video. The mother saw that the program was more violent and sexual than she wanted to watch, and turned it off. But a few days later her little daughter was raped by a group of boys whose parents had not turned off the program.

A TIME FOR ACTION

Through an organization called M.A.D.D., Mothers Against Drunk Driving, a group of women have gotten together to stiffen the drinking laws. They got mad at drunk driving, and they decided to do something about it. They started talking with other mothers, with other organizations, with the press, and with people of influence. They were angry about what was happening to their kids, and rightly so.

The number of kids killed by drunken drivers is small compared to the number who are being hooked on pornography, who are being seduced and deceived, who are being raped and abused and driven into prostitution, right now!

ENDNOTES

1. Congressman Lee H. Hamilton, quoted in *The Cincinnati Enquirer,* "Pornography," Sept. 20, 1984, A-18.

2. Galloway, "Crackdown on Pornography—A No-Win Battle," 84.

3. John H. Court, *Pornography: a Christian Critique* (Downers Grove, Ill.: Inter-Varsity, 1980), 86.

4. Laura Lederer, ed., *Take Back the Night* (New York: Morrow, 1980), 126.

5. A model cable law has been written by Morality In Media and is now being considered in the state of Florida under the leadership of Ms. Barbara Hattemer.

Chapter 4

Devastation for Women

The biggest disease today is not leprosy or tuberculosis, but rather the feeling of being unwanted, uncared for, and deserted by everybody. The greatest evil is the lack of love and charity, the terrible indifference toward one's neighbour who lives at the roadside assaulted by exploitation, corruption, poverty, and disease.
Mother Teresa of Calcutta, quoted by Malcolm Muggeridge in
Something Beautiful for God, 52-53

When *Playboy* magazine representatives visit the campuses looking for models for the annual feature, "Girls of the Big Ten," coeds literally line up in the streets for a chance to step inside to drop their clothes for the photographers, hoping to be chosen to pose nude in the magazine. Those who are picked will hold autograph parties at the bookstores, signing their pictures in the issue when it comes out on the market. They think it's great fun, an honor to be a *"Playmate."*

ALL THOSE PRETTY GIRLS

The accounts given by professional models are a far cry from the *Playboy* illusion of joy and fun. When *Penthouse* published compromising pictures of

Vanessa Williams, leading to her resignation as Miss America in 1984, she told the press, "This is the worst thing that ever happened to me." She felt "violated by *Penthouse*" because she had never consented to let the pictures be published.

After hearing about the *Penthouse* photos, her father said:

> The whole world passed before my eyes. I saw my friends. I saw the people at my job....What will they think of me? How will I be able to go back to work and hold my head high and feel comfortable with them again? Will they be looking at me every time I walk down the corridor? Will someone be staring at me and wondering?[1]

A porn star, who would not release her real name, described what the real world of pornography is like for the models: "As much as possible I tried to keep detached from the pictures, from how they were being taken, and where they were going....The jobs I hated most were the ones where you had to 'emote.' *Emote* means the guy would say something like 'Pretend you're really getting it,' or 'Make love to the camera.' "[2]

WOMEN:TOOLS OF THE TRADE

While men suffer deception and degradation from participation with pornography, the damage done to women who are exploited by the porn world—and women in general—is almost incalculable. This damage is often overlooked. Hear me: pornography inflicts injury, pain, and death on all it touches, but uniquely on women.

Physical abuse, filthy working conditions, and disease are taken for granted in the industry. Women who work in the pornography business often have vaginal trichomoniasis or some infection from the working conditions, which run from bad to intolerable. The communicable diseases like hepatitis and mononucleosis spread quickly.[3]

Proponents of pornography often point to Denmark, where the smut trade was legalized in 1969, as an example of the harmlessness of an unrestricted sex industry. But the individuals whose lives have been destroyed by mercenary exploitation speak differently.

The many women I talked to during my three months as a pornography model often hated themselves. But it was very often of bitter necessity that they did it. For me, too, it was almost impossible to get out again....Most of the male models think it is OK. But it's the women who have to be tied up, who have to do everything so that a man can get his....I learned quickly to hate my body and myself....And I learned, too, that it is men who have the upper hand in this situation.[4]

Victims in the exploitation films of the sixties and seventies and the hard-R slasher movies of the eighties are invariably women, assaulted, tortured, and degraded. The media presents the illusion that the model/actress really enjoys what is being done to her, and the public believes it.

Pretending to enjoy painful or disgusting acts has been required of prostitutes since sin began. Apparently the ability to disguise pain is also necessary for the women used to produce pornography. Although in certain films the models actually appear to be in pain, producers argue that this is only to arouse viewers and to convince them that the action is real. Usually, the action that was originally resisted by the female in these films—rape, beating, sadism—supposedly arouses her to the point where she begs for more abuse.[5]

The common attitude is that since the model/actress receives money for her services, she is a prostitute. This may be true. But the attitude is also that, short of outright murder, it's impossible to violate a prostitute, whether by cruelty, beating, or torture.

> One does not violate something by using it for what it is: neither rape nor prostitution is an abuse of the female because in both the female is fulfilling her natural function; that is why rape is absurd and incomprehensible as an abusive phenomenon in the male system, and so is prostitution, which is held to be voluntary even when the prostitute is hit, threatened, drugged, or locked in.[6]

Peep shows and live acts in adult bookstores in many large cities consist of nothing more than naked women on a revolving platform, exposing themselves and occasionally masturbating for the titillation of men who pay twenty-five cents for a three-minute gawk through a glass window. For fifty cents, some locations provide a private booth with a microphone, so the voyeur can speak to the model and maybe persuade her to do something special just for him. How do rational people deny that such obscenity is degrading to all women?

Read the books by women who have been wounded by pornography. I recommend *Take Back the Night*, although it is not pleasant reading. It reveals one of the most tragic effects of pornography—the shattering of young women's lives. Because of the pain they have suffered, they have generalized the mentality of the producers and distributors of filth onto all males and, as a result, find it impossible to have a caring relationship with any man. Will the Christian community respond to these women with condemnation? Or will we reach out to them with the love and healing of Jesus Christ?

WHY WORRY?

Why should the community be concerned if some people want to look at dirty magazines? Murray Strauss and Larry Baron, sociologists at the University of New Hampshire, discovered that there is "an unusually high correlation between sex magazine readership and the rape rate."

Datum for rape was taken from the annual F.B.I. Uniform Crime Reports. The study was based on the most widely read sexually oriented magazines including *Chic, Genesis, Hustler, Playboy*, and others. In summary, Strauss said that the "sex magazine readership index" was devised in order to determine to what extent sex magazines were part of the "popular culture" of each state. "This index was found to be highly correlated with the incidence of rape." Their findings were confirmed when the analysis was repeated a second year, and the association between rape and pornography remained the same in spite of careful measures to eliminate any outside influences that might have distorted their results.[7]

This study showed that Alaska and Nevada lead all

other states in readership of pornography in proportion to the population. Alaska and Nevada also have higher rape rates than all other states. Although the researchers stopped short of saying that sex magazine readership causes rape, the correlation is clear and the data certainly draw us toward no other conclusion.

THE PIT AND THE PEDESTAL

The threat of rape has become a fact of life in the eighties. The escalation of wife battering, sexual abuse of little children, and all categories of rape are increasing at a rate that far exceeds population growth. Since 1933 the rape rate in America has increased over 700 percent—and authorities tell us that this figure is small. Only one in four attempted or actual rapes is ever reported to the police.[8] Does this rise in rape have anything to do with the increasing availability and intensity of pornography which presents rape as desired by women?

Feminists such as Susan Brownmiller, Laura Lederer, and Kate Millett say emphatically, yes. Pornography is directly related to sexual violence toward women. Nearly all pornography, they say, is geared toward men and is filled with misogyny—hatred of women. Soft-porn magazines like *Playboy* and *Penthouse* dehumanize women with labels like *bunny* or *pet*, and by explicit or implied violence. Tenderness, commitment, any resemblance to romantic love are totally absent from their portrayal of sex. The sexual revolution liberates males to think of women as genitalia, available to any man, any time.

Fragmentation, a common photographic technique

picturing the mouth or sex organs separate from the whole body, discounts the personhood of the model. Women are conditioned to think of themselves as a marketable commodity, a "sweet thing"—an impersonal object to be consumed by a man. The names given to models often reflect that mentality: "Taffy," "Candy," or "Cookie." To the feminist, the acceptability of pornography is a clear statement about the acceptability of misogyny and of the real status of women in American society.[9]

Author Andrea Dworkin and others argue that pornography is creating a cultural climate in which a rapist feels he is merely giving in to a normal urge and women are expected to submit to rape and sadism as healthy liberated fun. Advocates of sexual freedom such as The Rene' Guyon Society typically support male freedom to use women indiscriminately.

"Every charge by women that force is used to violate women—in rape, battery, or prostitution—is dismissed by positing a female nature that is essentially fulfilled by the act of violation, which in turn transforms violation into merely using a thing for what it is and blames the thing if it is not womanly enough to enjoy what is done to it."[10] Stated more simply, if she can't relax and enjoy it, something's wrong with her.[11]

THE EXPERT OPINION

A flood of research by clinical psychologists and psychiatrists since 1970 consistently shows that this violent fantasy material can lead to changes in sexual attitudes, appetites, and behavior.

A typical experiment will stimulate a group of subjects with pornographic material, then give them an opportunity to "punish" an innocent person (a confederate in the research) with electric shocks. Their willingness to inflict pain on another is compared to a neutral group who were not exposed to the pornography.

If the pornography is very mild—pinups and cheesecake-type photos—it seems to dampen aggressiveness: the subject will be less willing to inflict pain on another person. But more graphic pornographic material regularly increases the subjects' willingness to harm their partners, especially when the material combines both erotic and violent elements.

> In the situation of reading about or witnessing a filmed presentation of rape—if the female victim is seen as in great pain, can also have a dampening effect on aggressive arousal. It serves as an inhibitor. But if the portrayal shows the woman as finally succumbing to and enjoying the act [typical of most pornography] then the situation is reversed for males [but not females]. It becomes very arousing. For men, the fantasy of a woman becoming sexually excited as a result of a sexual assault reverses any inhibitions that might have been initially mobilized by the coercive nature of the act and seeing the woman in pain.[12]

In an interview for *Action* Magazine, Christian psychologist John Drakeford explained the relationship between pornography and sexual violence:

> I believe that what you read today, you do tomorrow. Now just consider, what does a person read when he reads pornography? He reads that women want to be handled roughly in a sexual relationship. That's just not true. You talk to women; they don't want rough sexual partners.
>
> Take the recent situation in New Bedford, Massa-

chusetts. Several men raped a woman in a bar. I think these men really believed this is what the woman wanted. And where did they get this idea? Most likely they got it from pornographic presentations which show women enjoying being handled roughly—even being attacked.[13]

PROOF OF THE POISON

At the Symposium on Media Violence and Pornography held in Toronto in February 1984, Dr. Dolf Zillman presented the conclusions of a study which strongly indicated that pornography promotes the victimization of women.

The study used "standard fare" pornography (not particularly violent sexual scenes), containing fellatio, cunnilingus, intercourse in all conceivable positions, and anal intercourse. The material shown often included a third party, or group sex (common in commercial pornography), and was specifically chosen to portray no coercion, but mutual consent of the sexual participants.

The test subjects watched the pornography in six consecutive weekly sessions of six films per session. The subjects were further divided into three groups: the first viewed six pornographic films per session; the intermediate group viewed three pornographic and three "innocuous" films (containing no sexually arousing material) in each session, and the last group (as a control group) viewed only six "innocuous" films.

The viewers were then tested at intervals of one, two, and three weeks after the last viewing to assess the effects of pornography.

The viewers' arousal response to standard fare is

lost after repeated exposure; that is to say, ordinary explicit sexual material becomes boring. Furthermore, repeated exposure to standard fare removes revulsion to more bizarre material. The viewers developed an increased appetite for more bizarre sexual materials, along with boredom with standard fare.

These effects remained consistent two weeks after exposure. Additional studies confirm Zillman's findings and also build on the findings of a study done in 1971 by Howard, Reifler, and Liptzin.

Three weeks after viewing the pornographic films, Dr. Zillman and his associates tested the subjects for any further effects. They found that after massive exposure to pornography, the viewers had developed distorted perceptions of sexuality in others. The subjects thought of other individuals as being extremely active sexually, and that obscure sexual practices such as sadism and bestiality were common practices. Individuals who had not been exposed to the pornography showed none of these distorted perceptions.

The researchers found there was an enormous loss of concern about the ill effects of pornography. Once people had been massively exposed, they developed the attitude that pornography was not particularly offensive and not necessarily harmful to others, including minors.

A disturbing indication from these testings was the trivialization of rape. Men who had been massively exposed to pornography came to look at rape as "reasonable" or "trivial." They had begun to believe that rape wasn't so bad; in fact, it might be fun to try it. To many of them, rape was no longer a crime at all.

The thing that shocked us the most was that we found a similar effect among women. Even women who had been massively exposed to standard pornography came to look at rape as a trivial offense.

There can be no doubt that pornography, as a form of primarily male entertainment, promotes the victimization of women, in particular.[14]

On the other hand, some researchers have denied that pornography has a direct influence on violent sex crimes. In a study published in 1973, Michael Goldstein of U.C.L.A. reported the results of his investigation of seven categories of sexual deviants, comparing their use of pornography in early and later life and its apparent effect on their sexual behavior. Convicted rapists, pedophiles, transsexuals, and homosexuals were included, as well as college students as control subjects. From his data, Goldstein concluded that exposure to pornography prior to age seventeen has little effect on later sexual behavior, although use of obscene materials in adulthood did seem to coincide with deviance—but probably as a result of personal preference, not obsession.[15]

Examination of Goldstein's data, though, reveals some interesting figures. For example, when rapists were asked if they *desired* to imitate sexual acts seen in pornographic material, 35 percent said that they did as adults, and 80 percent did as youths. When asked if they actually *did* imitate sex acts seen in pornography, 15 percent confessed they had as adults, and 30 percent had as youths. And when asked if they performed some *other* sexual act after viewing pornography, 20 percent had as adults, and 25 percent had as youths. In 1973, Goldstein did not consider these percentages significant. How is that possible? Does his conclusion follow from the data?

THE FRACTURED FAMILY

Pornography destroys marriages. It leads to infidelity, sexual abuse, and divorce. It will come between husband and wife, when one will be so obsessed with the fantasies seen in the pages of a magazine that they can no longer experience the reality of normal sex with their spouse. An anonymous author—a man in full-time Christian ministry—described what pornography had done to his own marriage:

> [Lust for pornography] did not destroy my marriage, did not push me out to find more sexual excitation in an adulterous affair, or with prostitutes, did not even impel me to place unrealistic demands on my wife's sexual performance. The effect was far more subtle. Mainly, I think, it cumulatively caused me to devalue my wife as a sexual being. The great lie promulgated by *Playboy*, television commercials, and racy movies is that the physical ideal of beauty is attainable and oh, so close....
>
> I start to view my own wife in that light. I expect her to have Farrah's smile, Cheryl's voluptuousness, Angie's legs, Miss October's flaming red hair and sparkling eyes. Envy and greed join hands with lust. I begin to focus on my wife's minor flaws. I lose sight of the fact that she is a charming, warm, attractive woman and that I am fortunate to have found her.
>
> Beyond that, lust affected my marriage in an even more subtle and pernicious way. Over time, I began to view sex schizophrenically. Sex in marriage was one thing. We performed O.K., though not as often as I liked, and accompanied by typical misunderstand-

ings. But passion, ah, that was something different. Passion I never felt in my marriage.

If anything, sex within marriage served as an overflow valve, an outlet for the passion that mounted inside me, fed by sources kept hidden from my wife. We never talked about this, yet I am sure she sensed it. I think she began to view herself as a sex object...in the deprived sense of being only the object of my physical necessity and not of romance and passion.[16]

Sexuality is intended to deepen relationships. Pornography destroys relationships. It makes sex animal rather than human and relational. If communication is bad, sex will not be good. If affection within marriage is absent, then sex cannot be good.

Sexual intercourse is the God-given method for renewing wedding vows, and should be entered into with the same sensitivity and desire for self-giving love that was true on the wedding day. The reason many women are turned off by sex is because the sensitivity and love that the man revealed when he made those vows is no longer expressed. If affection within marriage is absent, then the sexual relationship cannot be mutual. The woman will feel used, because what makes her feel special is communication, tenderness, thoughtfulness, and being taken seriously. Pornography eliminates all these elements.

In many cases, the violence portrayed in pornography is acted out in the home. On September 1, 1984, the Knight-Ridder newspapers carried a report of a man who was convicted of kidnapping and raping his wife. He had beaten her on the head, bound her hands and feet with duct tape, then tied her to the posts of a bed with rope. How much common sense is needed to relate such crimes to the violence and bondage spewing out from the "adult" theaters and newsstands?

THE DESENSITIZATION OF MEN

What is pornography doing to men? Too many of us stand by and say, "Well, that's terrible, but I'm not a rapist or an abuser. I may look at pornography now and then, but I'm not addicted to it. I can take it or leave it." If that's your attitude, you're kidding yourself.

We've lost our sense of shame. The *Playboy* philosophy has distorted our thinking to the point where we can't tell right from wrong. The very attitude that says, "I can look at it and it doesn't bother me," is evidence that the harm has already been done. Neutralization has begun.

Dr. Victor Cline of the University of Utah, has specialized for many years in the treatment of sexual deviances, and states that the use of pornography can have four distinct effects:

1. *Addiction*—The user develops a powerful need to view and consume the material, losing free control of his own behavior.

2. *Escalation*—The user develops a tolerance for milder material, requiring progressively "rougher" pictorial and verbal material to achieve the same arousal.

3. *Desensitization*—The user will no longer feel repulsion for sexual deviances, and develops a *loss of compassion* for the victim being raped or beaten.

4. *Acting out*—Fantasizing very likely becomes overt behavior.[17]

We must treat sin as absolutely intolerable. Recently I had to confront a man who abused his wife, hit her, and blackened her eye. "She makes me so mad," he said. "She nags and carries on till I can't stand it, and I let her have it. It's happened a couple times before, but she's really asking for it by the way she treats me."

"Intolerable!" I told him. "Absolutely intolerable! If you'd come to me the first time, the likelihood of its happening again would have been greatly reduced." He faced the fact of his sin, his responsibility both for his violent action and for shifting the blame to his wife.

Pornography is destructive to men. It causes us to be irresponsible, to separate the pretty face of the model from the face of the daughter, the sister, the human soul that's behind the pretty face. It teaches men to think of women in terms of genitalia, or as objects to be used and then discarded.

Edward Donnerstein and Neil Malamuth found that exposure to pornography that mixes sex with violence had six definite effects:

1. It sexually excites and arouses (especially) the male viewer.

2. It increases both his aggressive attitudes and behavior.

3. It stimulates the production of aggressive rape fantasies.

4. It increases men's acceptance of so-called rape myths ("Women ask for it").

5. It produces a lessened sensitivity about rape (and increases callousness).

6. It leads to men's admitting an increased possibility of themselves' raping someone—especially if they think they can get away with it.[18]

The Christian tradition has not needed clinical research to understand that sex separated from modesty and tenderness must be brutal. From the first century on, the church has argued for the sanctity of loving sex within marriage, for the good of both man and woman.

If you are involved in any way—even casually or passively—with the reading and viewing of pornographic material, I beg you in the name of Jesus Christ our Lord: *Turn from it at once.* Resolve this moment to make a clean break from whatever involvement you may have. Ask God to cleanse and forgive you, to empower you to say a firm and final no to any attraction to pornographic material both now and forever.

ENDNOTES

1. "Ex-Miss America Endures Pain, Embarrassment Sparked By Flap Over Nude Pictures," *Jet,* August 6, 1984, 60-62.

2. Laura Lederer, *Take Back the Night* (New York: William Morrow, 1980), 63.

3. Ibid., 66.

4. Ibid., 84.

5. George N. Gordon, *Erotic Communications* (New York: Hastings House, 1980), 111.

6. Andrea Dworkin, *Pornography* (New York: G.P. Putnam's Sons, 1981), 204.

7. L. Baron, and M. A. Strauss, "Sexual Stratification, Pornography and Rape" in N.M. Malamuth and E. Donnerstein, ed., *Pornography and Sexual Aggression* (New York: Academic, 1984).

8. Victor B. Cline, "Aggression Against Women: the Facilitating Effects of Media Violence and Erotica" (Paper delivered at meeting of the associated students of the University of Utah, Salt Lake City, April 8, 1983), 17.

9. Lederer, 62.

10. Dworkin, 205.

11. In 1984, researchers M.H. Silbert and A.M. Pines studied 200 prostitutes, finding 193 cases of rape. In roughly one quarter of the attacks, the rapist appeared to be acting out behavior learned in pornography. In one incident, the attacker said, "I seen it all in the movies—you love being beaten. You know you love it, tell me you love it." Press, "The War Against Pornography," 65.

12. Cline, 21.

13. "Gaining Perspective," *Action*, July-August, 1984, 5-6.

14. D. Zillman and J. Bryant, *Pornography and Sexual Aggression* (New York: Academic, 1984), 115-138.

J.L. Howard, C.B. Reifer, and M.B. Liptzin, *Technical Report of the Commission on Obscenity and Pornography*, 8 (1971), (Washington, D.C.: U.S. Government Printing Office, 1971), 97-169.

D. Zillman, "Pornography, Sexual Callousness, and the Trivialization of Rape," *Journal of Communication*, Vol. 32 (4), 10-21.

K.E. Leonard and S.P. Taylor, "Exposure to Pornography, Permissive and Nonpermissive Cues, and Male Aggression toward Females," *Motivation and Emotion*, 7, 1983, 291-299.

D. Zillman, *Connection Between Sex and Aggression* (Hillsdale, N.J.: Laurence-Erlbaum, 1984).

Florence Schume, *Abnormal Psychology* (Lexington, Mass.: D.C. Heath, 1983), 434-435.

Albert Bandura, *Principles of Behavior Modification* (New York: Holt, 1969).

15. Michael Goldstein, "Exposure to Erotic Stimuli and Sexual Deviance," *American Journal of Social Issues*, 29, no. 3 (1973), 197.

16. "The War Within: An Anatomy of Lust," *Leadership*, 4 (1982), 38.

17. Cline, 23.

18. Cline, 23. See also N.M. Malamuth and E. Donnerstein in L. Berkowitz (ed.), *Advances in Experimental Social Psychology* vol. 15 (New York: Academic).

Chapter 5

Child Pornography: the Millstone

Woe to the world for temptations to sin!...See that you do not despise one of these little ones; for I tell you that in heaven their angels always behold the face of my Father who is in heaven....So it is not the will of my Father who is in heaven that one of these little ones should perish (Matt. 18:7, 10, 14).

You have heard that it was said, "You shall love your neighbor and hate your enemy." But I say to you, Love your enemies and pray for those who persecute you, so that you may be sons of your Father who is in heaven; for He makes His sun to rise on the evil and on the good, and sends rain on the just and on the unjust (Matt.5:43-44).

When Jesus tells us to love our enemies, He Himself will give us the love with which to do it. We are neither factories nor reservoirs of His love, only channels. When we understand that, all excuse for pride is eliminated.

Corrie ten Boom, *Amazing Love*, 27

One of the most difficult experiences of my ministry came the day I visited a young mother in our congregation. Her two little boys had been sexually molested—raped by a man in our community. I had to fight against rage. How could anyone be so sick as to assault little children?

In the last few years, it has become all too clear that this particular molester was but one individual in a burgeoning stampede of child molesters. Worse, they've been here for years and we didn't know it. We have been blind, and our children have paid the price of our blindness.

The Justice Department estimates that four thousand children in America are sexually abused and then murdered each year. Child pornography is a two-to-three-billion-dollar business annually, just in the United States. The material is marketed for pedophiles, for their voyeuristic gratification and to show to children in order to lure them into similar sexual activity. And it is also used by incestuous parents who seduce their own children.

Attorney Charles Keating, founder of Citizens for Decency through Law, has given sobering testimony on child molestation before the Senate Judiciary Committee. "Police vice squads report that 77 percent of child molesters of boys and 87 percent of child molesters of girls admitted trying out the sexual behavior modeled by pornography," Keating said.

In one group of rapists, 57 percent indicated they had tried out the sexual behavior they had seen depicted by pornography. One of the many specific examples Keating offered was of seven Oklahoma teen-age males who gang-attacked a fifteen-year-old female from Texas, forcing her to commit unnatural acts. Four of the teen-agers admitted being incited to commit the act by reading porn magazines and looking at lewd photographs.

According to *The Death of Innocence* by Sam Janus, only one childhood rape case in two hundred results in an arrest. Of that small number, less than 4 percent spend any time in jail. All the rest are dismissed or receive counseling or help from social agencies.

F.B.I. data show that one in four twelve-year-old girls in the United States will be sexually assaulted in her lifetime. The figures are only slightly lower for boys, and vary somewhat in different geographic areas. There seems to be greater danger on the West Coast and in large urban areas, although no area of the country is any longer considered safe.

Voices, an organization for incest survivors, estimates that 75 percent of young prostitutes have been sexually abused as children. In testimony before a U.S. Senate hearing in 1984, *Voices* spokeswoman Sandra Butler declared that women working in the pornography industry are "our people." What she means is that many, many of these women were sexually molested as children. "We're looking at a chain of abuse, and pornography is a critical link in the chain."[1]

Dr. Shirley O'Brien, University of Arizona human development specialist, estimates as many as six hundred thousand children—boys and girls as young as three years and as old as eighteen, but primarily ten- to sixteen-year-olds—are kidnapped, seduced, sexually molested, and photographed to produce child pornography each year. Many parents are shocked to learn that their children have been photographed for pornography by the "nice man [or woman] down the street."

Citizens for Decency through Law reports that there are about 260 different child-pornography magazines sold in this country. Between 1979 and 1982, the United States Customs Service officials seized more than 247,000 pieces of porn, of which 70 percent contained child porn.

THE SUBTLETY OF THE SERPENT

In my opinion, *Playboy* and the *Playboy* philosophy have helped to open the way for the spread of child pornography in the last thirty years. While maintaining a self-righteous aloofness to explicit molestation, *Playboy* nonetheless plays heavily on the theme. One technique is to use photographs of women dressed as children or imitating children and their behavior. The April 1976 cover had a very young-looking model dressed as a child, surrounded by teddy bears and rag dolls. The word *virgin* appeared nearby. In the September 1984 issue, the playmate of the month is shown rollerskating with a very small girl. Both the playmate and her "half-sister" are wearing extremely short skirts. In another photo, the playmate is pictured, scantily dressed, playing with two children. In this same issue, another naked model is posed masturbating with a china doll and a cherub statue.

Another favorite theme in the "quality men's magazines" is the use of perverted fairy tales in cartoons: Snow White is being raped by the dwarves, Goldilocks in bed with baby bear, Santa Claus's sexually abusing a reindeer or an elf or a child sitting on his lap. Cartoons from *Hustler* are far more graphic than those from *Playboy*, and tend to include blasphemy, while *Penthouse* seems to specialize in blood-and-gore cartoons relating to children.

Most individuals are repulsed by an overt picture of child molestation. But placed in a context that treats a vicious crime as a joke, "all in good fun," it becomes acceptable. The reader is gradually conditioned to accept the idea of children as sex objects.

RIPPLE EFFECT

Ann Wolbert Burgess, associate director of nursing research for the Boston Department of Health and Hospitals, says that the public is becoming desensitized to the thought of youngsters as sex objects. In an address at the third annual Sexual Abuse Conference, Dr. Burgess cited two examples of child pornography in advertising. A naked little girl was used in an advertisement for men's shirts in *Gentlemen's Quarterly*. What would cause a magazine aimed primarily at affluent professional men to use a naked child to sell shirts? The second example Burgess mentioned showed a six-year-old girl, heavily made up and nude above the waist, advertising perfume in *Vogue*. *Harper's Bazaar*, December 1983, featured four full-page photos of a beautiful little girl, maybe 6 years old, naked from the chest up, handling bottles of popular perfumes.

Other publications are not so subtle. *Bambina Sex* and other underground publications from Denmark graphically display grown men fondling naked children—boys or girls according to each magazine's specialty—ejaculating onto their backs or stomachs, forcing sex organs into their mouths. One film seemed to show a man pressing himself into a six-year-old girl, while she cried in pain. Can you imagine the effect of this horror on the children? Or the effect on adults who see it? What will be the effect on our children and grandchildren as this alters the attitude toward child abuse in our society?

These statistics speak clearly: of inmates in penal institutions, 70 percent were sexually abused in childhood.[2] Of female teen-age prostitutes on the street, 75 percent have experienced rape, incest, or molestation earlier in their lives.[3]

These figures are terrifying in themselves. But just stop and think—if the number of children now being sexually abused is growing, the number of victimizers in the next generation will grow as well.

The incidence of pregnancy among girls aged nine to fifteen has increased dramatically. Some of these victims have never had a menstrual period. Their little bodies are not ready to bear the stress of carrying a baby to full-term, and the physical trauma of the pregnancy and birth experience can prevent their bearing healthy babies later in life. Rectal bleeding from sexual abuse can be fatal. Gonorrhea of the throat can suffocate; herpes and syphilis can leave lifelong infections and emotional scars.

Pediatrician Elizabeth Holland, a vital Christian, tells of a boy who had been systematically raped by his father every weekend since the child had been two years old. "This four-year-old little boy's rectum looked like hamburger meat." Another case, a three-year-old, had a draining sore on his penis. Further investigation revealed that the mother had been having vaginal intercourse with her son. The child had venereal disease.

"I can cure venereal disease," says Dr. Holland. "I can stitch up the lacerations and put ointment on the wounds. But I cannot touch the damage and the scars that have been inflicted on the minds, and hearts, and spirits of these little ones."

In other cases, sexual abuse is not as visible as other forms of violent abuse. In the NBC television special, "The Silent Shame," Dr. Bruce Woodling described the necessity for physicians using specialized instruments to find the tiny abrasions and scars in the genital area that can corroborate a child's testimony when more apparent evidence is missing. The tragedy is, too many physicians do not take the time to look carefully, to question the child privately. Too often, the doctor does not want to get involved following through with the legal steps that could remove the child from further danger.

Father Bruce Ritter of Covenant House on Times Square says that most kids working the street for pornographers and pimps last about a year before turning up dead in the trunk of a car, in the river, or in the gutter. Many of the young people die prematurely from the effects of the alcohol and drugs they invariably use to dull the emotional pain of their lives. In many cases, the victims of pornographers are simply murdered when they are no longer useful.

A large percentage of the photographing of sexual acts by children is done by individual child molesters. However, most child-porn magazines are professionally photographed by those working in or for the porn syndicates. Citizens for Decency Through Law believes that the syndicate farms out this dangerous work but controls its output and distribution. Therefore, we believe that child porn will never be stopped without putting legal heat on those in the adult pornography syndicate.

Bruce Taylor of Citizens for Decency Through Law agrees. "You'll never get rid of child porn until you get rid of the general pornography industry. It's the same people producing it. If the federal government is serious about wiping out kiddie porn, it ought to put the producers and distributors in jail.

"Child porn is the most secretive area of the pornography industry. But when you get the porno syndicate, and shut off the commercial market which is creating the appetite for child pornography, then you'll make the child porn go under. If you really want to get rid of it, you have to hit at the roots of the problem."

SICK UNTO DEATH

Special agent Kenneth Lanning of the Behavioral Science Unit of the F.B.I. Academy, notes that too often discussions and research on pornography focus on the effects on the viewer rather than on the effects on the child subject. Children used in pornography, Lanning says, are desensitized and conditioned to respond as sexual objects. They are ashamed and embarrassed about their portrayal in such material. The permanency, longevity, and circulation of the record of their sexual abuse causes great anxiety in the children, who often commit crimes of theft or setting fires in futile attempts to destroy what they think is evidence of their guilt. Lanning continues,

> Child pornography...can be defined as the sexually explicit reproduction of a child's image, voice, or handwriting. In essence, it is the permanent record of the sexual abuse of a child. The only way you can produce child pornography is to sexually molest a child. Child pornography exists only for the consumption of pedophiles.[4]

A pedophile will use the photographs or films to blackmail the victim, saying that he will show the pictures to the child's parents if the secret is told. Other children may be seduced by being shown the pictures and told, "See, other kids do this, so it's okay." The pictures are also traded between pedophiles, and many of the materials eventually are sold to producers of commercial child pornography.[5]

The psychological damage is serious long-term. Often children report that they were given drugs to help them relax and smile prettily while being photographed. Children molested at Isabel's Nursery School in Los Angeles still have nightmares several years after the abuse was discovered and stopped. One little boy cries out in the dark, "He's going to kill me! If I tell, he'll cut me up!" Others withdraw, avoiding all social contact.

Ann Burgess says that the secrecy demanded by pornographers causes children to assume guilt, feeling that they are rejected by society, and that they are most likely to develop antisocial behavior such as chemical abuse or sexual deviance themselves.[6]

Without exception, police find that pedophiles and molesters have drawers or file cases stuffed with hundreds of pictures of little boys or girls—either commercial pornography, or photos they have made themselves, or both. Many of the commercial publications come through Denmark, Holland, or Sweden. More and more material, though, is now thought to be produced in the United States, then distributed through a post-office box in Denmark. Still others are products of the Third World.

> You can find this child pornography in the most elegant and chic parts of Stockholm, as well as in the poorer sections of town. There are pictures of small black children with gigantic penises in their mouths....It is easier to exploit or abuse Asian

children....these children are sold for pornographic purposes because it is considered more exotic for white men to have sex with children who are not white. The final reason for this specialization is, of course, so that one does not identify that girl in the picture with one's own daughter.[7]

A pedophile featured on "The Silent Shame" described his insidious method. If it only happens once, the child might tell. But if he can get her to do it again, then he will threaten her. "You did it twice, so you must have liked it. If you tell, it will be your fault." So the children don't tell, and the molester feels free to do with the child as he likes. This method of intimidation-producing silence is repeated in numerous studies and books.[8]

Convicted child molester Warren K. Mumpower presented his side of the story in a letter to a U.S. Senate committee investigating child abuse. He says he wants loving relationships with children, different, in his opinion, from rapists and other molesters. He blames parents, especially single parents, for failing to demonstrate affection to their children, leaving them lonely and vulnerable to pedophiles. "The pedophile's experiences with his girls are, in his mind, romantic experiences, and he may truly believe he is in love with her....Have you hugged your kids today? If not, a child molester will!"

DISPOSABLE KIDS

Pedophiles tend to love only children of a particular age. As long as a child fits the profile, the adult will give him or her constant attention and sexual favors. He really believes that he loves the child, and often the child becomes emotionally attached to him. But when the child becomes too old—maybe eight or maybe twelve, or perhaps when body hair or a beard begin to develop—then the pedophile loses interest, and the romance is over. The object of his "love" becomes just another throw-away kid, experiencing total rejection which heightens the child's experience of guilt, shame, and worthlessness.

THE ULTIMATE BETRAYAL

Dr. David New, a Christian psychologist, reports that increasing numbers of cases involving incest, especially father/daughter incest, are appearing in his counseling practice. He has identified six common factors which characterize almost every case:

1. A strained relationship between husband and wife.

2. Mother and daughter were not close, and often in open conflict.

3. Because of factors 1 and 2, daughter was insecure, longed for expressions of warmth, love, and acceptance. Accustomed to doing exactly as she was told, she becomes vulnerable.

4. Fathers worked variable schedules; mothers worked, leaving fathers alone with daughters regularly.

5. In each case, father was heavily into pornography prior to initiating aberrant behavior. Law enforcement officers report that they routinely find pornographic materials when investigating sexually abused children.

6. The daughters were filled with guilt and fearful of reporting the cause.

Dr. Holland describes her work with sexually

abused children in her private practice:

"I have treated in my office a family of four children. They were brought in by a distraught mother. It appeared that she had found pornography in her fourteen-year-old son's bedroom. There was a fourteen-year-old boy, a twelve-year-old girl, an eleven-year-old girl, and an eight-year-old boy in this family.

"This fourteen-year-old boy had been reading porn in his bedroom at night, until he was so sexually stimulated that he could no longer control himself, and would go into the bedrooms of his sisters and brother, and rape them several times weekly. This had been going on for five years, since the eldest boy was eight years old...his youngest brother had been three years old at the time he had begun to be visited several times weekly for sexual intercourse by this then eight-year-old brother."

In another case, Dr. Holland recalls: "I treated in my office a four-year-old little girl who had a torn and lacerated vagina. It seems that her father and uncles and brothers shared pornography among themselves. And after arousing themselves, they took turns sexually abusing this little girl, passing her back and forth among themselves.

"Do you know what I found, to my horror? I found that this little girl had been taken to another physician when she was three; same symptoms, same history. But this doctor chose to close his eyes to what was happening in this little girl's life. He prescribed ointment for the physical injury, and he sent her back into the situation from which she came. And because of his indifference, this child endured another year of torture and pain and fear at the hand of those God gave her to protect her.

"Who's to blame for this child? The father? The uncles? The brothers? Of course. But what about the one who saw and understood, yet chose to look the other way?"

What about the people who produce and distribute the pornographic material? What about the community store where it is sold? What about the general public who support the illicit sex industry either by buying the material, supporting the advertisers who use sex to sell their products, or who merely walk on the other side of the street and do nothing?

True, we are not directly to blame. But if we are called to love, now that we know the facts, can any of us be blameless in the future?

Dr. Holland goes on to say, "I am told by psychologists and sociologists that I have no right to speak out against pornography, that the statistics don't show any link between pornography and sexual abuse. They may be right about the statistics; I don't know, because I've spent the last ten years treating the victims, not studying research papers. But I know that the statistics on paper don't count. I treat the real statistics in my office. I put my hands in their wounds, I see the fear and bewilderment in the little children and the teen-agers. I *know* there is a link with pornography."

Father Bruce Ritter of Covenant House blames the plight of today's youth not only on the pornographers or those who distribute smut, but the entire nation of adults who silently support the system by patronizing stores which sell porn and by buying products that are marketed with sexual images. In his message to the National Consultation on Pornography in Cincinnati, 1984, Father Ritter stated clearly that it's not the kids who are the problem, but us, the complacent adults.

"We are the problem. We reward those who use sex. We have succeeded in almost completely separating sex from love, stability, fidelity, and children. The most popular shows on commercial television mock the concepts of transcendence, of love and fidelity, of nurturing and cherishing, which must be the basis of true sexuality.

"The kids are the victims. Not just the runaways or prostitutes, although they are certainly victims. But the tens of millions of kids who are consumers of the products marketed in this 'sex-for-sale society.' They get the message over and over that it's O.K. to pay for sex."

After all, it's the adults that pander obscenity to youth, provide the money, market the products, encourage the "rock culture" for the capitalistic gold mine that it is. Few young people are mature enough to realize that they are being led on for monetary gain, and few of their parents do more than ignore or condemn the current fad.

THE FRONT PORCH OF HADES

Have you seen the rock videos on cable TV? They are packed with bloody violence mixed with bizarre sexual images, demonism, suicide, and death. Fantasies of chained or caged women are a favorite feature of MTV. It's the "in thing" for the young people. In this unholy marriage of rock music and the film industry, the mercenaries are getting rich and the young people are being slaughtered by immorality and violence.

So you won't think that I am exaggerating, I want to repeat what the rock culture says about itself. Bob Ezrin, the producer for Kiss, is quoted in *Rolling*

Stone describing Kiss as "symbols of unfettered evil and sensuality." *Rock* magazine calls Kiss "fire-breathing demons from rock and roll." Again, from *Rolling Stone*: "Peter Criss boldly declares, 'I find myself evil! I believe in the devil as much as in God. You can use either one to get things done.' "[9] At concerts, Kiss will leap onto the stage, spew "blood" from their mouths, screaming words to the effect that "we'll steal your virgin soul!"

If Kiss were unique, we might dismiss their antics as simply perverse showmanship; but they aren't unique. *Newsweek* called Mick Jagger "the Lucifer of Rock," "the unholy roller" and spoke of his demonic power to affect people.[10] Kiss, the Rolling Stones (the band), and Black Sabbath are three of several rock bands that are blatantly satanic. Whether they present themselves as demonic because of authentic belief or simply as a marketing ploy is academic—they are advertising evil, and our young people are buying it in a big way.

Prince (star of "Purple Rain") performs live on stage in a purple trench coat and black lace panties, or he may thrill his audiences by pulling open his shirt and the top of his tight-fitting pants, exposing his pubic hair to the young crowd. One of his group came close to being arrested in Cincinnati at his concert in 1985.

Rock music is closely related to the film industry. Kiss star Gene Simmons took off his demonic makeup to play a homicidal maniac named Charles Luther in the movie "Runaway," directed by Michael Crichton. "He's like Darth Vader without the mask," says Gene. "The best part is I get to do scenes with all the women in the cast." When Prince made his movie debut in R-rated "Purple Rain," reviewer Scot Haller described the film as "misogyny, rivaling that of the most outrageous anti-woman videos,...like nothing seen on the big screen this year."[11] Even the Jacksons have a video for their hit tune "Torture" that shows a masked woman flailing a whip.[12]

Investigate for yourself. Walk into a record shop and flip through the album covers in the rock music section. Look at the faces and the costumes. Look at the graphics and the "decorative" illustrations. How many albums portray violence, hatred, ugliness? How many depict the demonic? How many show romance or tenderness, compared to those that show the dark side of sexuality? What is the mentality that believes such stuff is marketable? And make no mistake...it is making big money!

Lyrics are sometimes printed on the back covers or dust-covers of albums. Look at "1999," by Prince, described in the *New York Tribune* as "lewd, vulgar, extremely explicit...heard between the beats [music] were obscene words and sounds simulating intercourse."[13] Or listen to the LP version of "Miracles" by Jefferson Starship. The actual words are too offensive to quote, but frequently describe crude oral sex, brutality, and perversion. Judas Priest merits special mention for its extremely graphic sadomasochistic themes: "music to kill your parents by."

Is there any relationship between what we see in the rock culture and the statistics that show teen-age suicide has skyrocketed in recent years? News reports in February 1985, ranked suicide as the second leading cause of teen-age deaths in the United States; it has tripled in the last twenty-five years.[14]

If we believe that radio and television are valuable

educational tools; if communities invest in public television for its educational impact; if Christians invest in both radio and television because of its power to effect those who listen and watch; if classical literature, music, and art can lift the spirit and inspire greatness, why can't we also see that violent sexual magazines, lewd programming, and degrading music are also powerfully educational in a dark and terrible way?

WHO IS THE STUMBLING BLOCK?

Jesus said, "Whoever receives one such child in my name receives me; but whoever causes one of these little ones who believe in me to sin, it would be better for him to have a great millstone fastened round his neck and to be drowned in the depth of the sea" (Matt. 18:5-6).

Who is responsible for causing the "little ones" of our communities to sin through pornography? Should we blame the pornographers who produce it, or the pimps who lead models to submit to it? Perhaps we should blame the exhibitionists who are willing to perform lewd acts in public, or maybe the distributors and retail outlet owners who profit from the lust of the consumer.

Perhaps we need to go a few steps further in identifying the stumbling blocks. What about the people who purchase it, creating a market in which pornography flourishes? Surely they are responsible. And how about the advertisers who use pornography as a way of enlarging their product markets? Or consider the prosecutors who don't enforce the law. Aren't they to blame for the proliferation of criminal activity?

But why stop there? What about the apathetic public that does not demand that the prosecutors enforce the law? How about A.C.L.U. lawyers (many of whom have received support directly from the "Playboy Foundation") who have fought for the "rights" of the pornographers, ignoring the rights of decent citizens?

And what about Christians who confess that "Jesus is Lord," who feel uneasy about what they see on the newsstands, who never or seldom view indecency themselves, but who lack faith to believe that God could use them to change the situation? Or perhaps those of us who don't love the victims enough to want to help? Or Christians who don't want to be different or stand up and be counted, who are fearful of being laughed at by their friends? Which of these are the stumbling block to the little ones of the nation?

Certainly all of the above.

"Not every one who says to me, 'Lord, Lord,' shall enter the kingdom of heaven, but he who does the will of my Father who is in heaven" (Matt. 7:21). Because Jesus Christ loves the children, let us commit ourselves to turn back the onslaught of pornography.

"Making an open stand against the ungodliness and unrighteousness which overspreads our land as a flood, is one of the noblest ways of confessing Christ in the face of His enemies," counseled John Wesley, (Garth Lean, *Strangely Warmed*, Tyndale, 1979, 62).

TIME TO BE ANGRY

It's easy to be overwhelmed with rage at the destruction of these innocents. I spoke about child pornography at a morning men's group, and afterward a man who is a long-time Christian came up to me. "If I found that some creep had done that to my grand-daughter, I'd take my hunting gun and kill him!"

I rebuked his violence, but not his anger. Anger is good, because it puts the fire within us to do something to end the exploitation of children, to stop the pornography. What difference does it make whether it's Joe's granddaughter, or my granddaughter, your own son, or your neighbor's baby? As long as *any* child is being abused, we *must* be angry, angry enough to take action, but we must not be overcome with rage that neutralizes our effectiveness and commitment to action.

When I was faced with the man who had allegedly molested the small boys, when he had a name and a face, it was different. Instead of raging against a "monster who had raped two little boys," I saw a broken man with deep problems, a man who had been mistreated in his own childhood, and who carried a crippling load of bitterness and self-hatred. I was angry with him, and I confronted him with his sin without hesitation, but I also wanted to help him, to bring him to a place where he could be healed. And, praise God, I have seen that man healed by the grace and love of Jesus Christ and God's people.

Our Lord said it would be better for one who led a little child into sin to have a millstone tied around his neck and cast into the sea. It's true. The judgment of God will be a terrible thing for unrepentant and unhealed molesters. But He didn't tell his disciples to go get the millstones.

ENDNOTES

1. Katherine Brady, testimony before the Senate Subcommittee on Juvenile Justice, U.S. Senate, Washington, D.C., August 8, 1984, 5.

Child Pornography: the Millstone

2. A. Nicholas Groth, interviewed on "The Silent Shame," NBC-TV, Aug. 25,1984. Dr. Groth is director of the Sex Offender Program at the Connecticut Correctional Institution, Somers, and author of *Men Who Rape*.

3. Jennifer James and Debra Boyer, "Entrance into Juvenile Prostitution" (Research paper supported by National Institute of Mental Health grant MH 29968, August 1980).

4. Ken Lanning, testimony before the Hearing Concerning Sexually Explicit Publications, U.S. Senate Subcommittee on Juvenile Justice, Washington, D.C., August 8, 1984, 3.

5. Ibid., 8.

6. Rita Rooney, "Innocence for Sale," *Ladies' Home Journal*, April 1983, 128.

7. Laura Lederer, *Take Back the Night* (New York: William Morrow, 1980), 87.

8. Lloyd Martin and Jill Haddad, *We Have a Secret* (Newport Beach, Calif: Crown Summit Books, 1982). Detective Lloyd Martin founded the Foundation for America's Sexually Exploited Children, Inc.

Shirley O'Brien, *Child Pornography* (Dubuque, Iowa: Kendall/Hunt Publishing Co., 1983).

Judianne Densen-Gerber and S. Hutchinson, "Medical-Legal and Societal Problems Involving Children" in *The Maltreatment of Children*, Selwyn Smith, ed. (Baltimore: University Park, 1978), 317-350.

9. Charles M. Young, "KISS," *Rolling Stone*, April 7, 1977, 49.

10. Rebecca Bricker, "Take One," *Newsweek*, January 4, 1971, 44.

11. *People*, August 6, 1984, 23.

12. Press, "The War Against Pornography," 61.

13. "Parents Urged to Hear Rock Music's Anti-Christian Message," *NFD Journal*, January 1985, 21.

14. "Certain pornographic magazines have illustrated fetishist ways to stimulate oneself autoerotically: demonstrations of how to hang oneself by a woman's stockings or slip, just long enough to become aroused...a practice that has resulted in hundreds of 'accidental' suicides." Charles Keating, Jr. (Statement at National Conference on Obscenity, Scottsdale, Arizona, Nov. 30, 1981).

PART II
Action Plan for Change

Chapter 6

The Starting Place

Prayer is likely to be undervalued by all but wise people because it is so silent and so secret. We are often deceived into thinking that noise is more important than silence. War sounds far more important than the noiseless growing crop of wheat; yet the silent wheat feeds millions, while war destroys them.

Frank Laubach, *Prayer, the Mightiest Force in the World*, 54

It would be wrong to show you the horror of pornography and to call you to fight against it at great personal cost, without equipping you with the tools necessary to join the battle, and to win. In this and the following chapters are specific tools, used in Cincinnati and in other cities, that have proven to be powerful and effective against the forces of obscenity. These tools can be used by an individual, or by large or small groups in any community of the United States, and in any other democracy where citizens have the power to influence their governing bodies.

This chapter and Chapter 9 will focus on the individual, while Chapter 10 will describe the tools that are particularly applicable to organized groups of committed citizens. I cannot overstate the importance of building a team as a base of operation. In fact, until you are fully committed to building a team against pornography, you are not ready to fight pornography at all. It is too difficult and too dangerous to face alone. The effectiveness of individual efforts will be limited, but those effects will be multiplied many times over by working as a team and speaking with a clear united voice. A beautiful example of this has developed in Columbia, South Carolina, and is described much more fully in Chapter 11.

Having said that, I must also say that it is possible to act decisively against pornography while you are building the team. With these tools you can act as an individual, or with two or three others, to immediately strengthen the rapidly growing movement against pornography and obscenity. This movement is growing daily across the country with leadership springing up in almost every community. I want to remind you that almost every movement begins with one or two persons' catching a vision and seeking to put that vision into practice. You may be that leader in your community. Don't underestimate what God is willing to do through you.

THE CENTRALITY OF PRAYER

If we are going to win the battle each of us face as committed Christians, and to help win the war that is raging across the country, we must start with prayer. Please don't skip over this section by assuming that you already understand this. This is not a tip of the hat to the pietists, nor an unnecessary detour in the battle plan. In fact, there is no area in my life where I am in greater need of growth. But we must face the facts. Prayer is the power cell for everything that we want to see happen. We cannot salvage one life through our own strength, let alone pick up the pieces of a generation already ravaged by the sexual revolution. Nor can we protect the next generations.

When we honestly and realistically face the true dimensions of the task ahead we are driven to pray. No one can face the depth of brokenness in each life, what it takes to heal even one victim, and the rapidly escalating numbers of women and children who are victims of violent sexual abuse and indecent sexual exposure, without being driven to pray. When we know that we cannot accomplish the task, cannot fix it, cannot make it right in our own strength, we are driven by God's Holy Spirit to pray with new intensity and new consistency.[1]

This happens in the lives of those who seriously take the time to understand what is happening in the lives of people through pornography. God is calling His people to righteousness. God is calling His people to the kind of prayer that produces righteousness within and righteousness through us.

THE POWER CELL

We must not only face the depth of the problem, we also need to grasp and be grasped by the love of God and the greatness and power of God. We need to see His willingness to use us and our prayers to make a difference. We need more than quick off-the-cuff prayers of the moment, more than conscience-easer prayers at the end of the day. We need people of prayer, people who are committed to becoming prayer warriors. We need people who are dissatisfied with the shallow and superficial experience of prayer that they have known in the past.

The Mind Polluters

The desperate suffering and needs of people around the world should drive us to our knees. By necessity, we have focused in this book on the devastation of the sexual revolution and pornography and sounded a call to righteousness—personal and national. But please keep in mind that concerned Christians must not only be concerned about the moral crisis, but must be equally concerned for the dignity and quality of life for all persons. We need a new vision for the worldwide human needs for food and safety, for jobs and for resources and justice. The needs are very real and urgent. But at the heart of all of this must be our continual focus on the call to righteousness.

Richard Foster begins *Celebration of Discipline* with these words: "Superficiality is the curse of our age. The doctrine of instant satisfaction is a primary spiritual problem. The desperate need today is not for a greater number of intelligent people, or gifted people, but for deep people."[2]

This is especially true in the area of prayer. As Foster states, prayer catapults us into the frontier of spiritual life, because it is "original research into unexplored territory."[3]

Prayer changes us because it brings us into the very presence of God. In that holy place, God not only reveals Himself to us, but also reveals the hiding places within us that need to change in order for God to use us as He wants to use us.

Through the centuries, men and women who have walked with God have made prayer the main business of their lives. Often when we think of Christian heroes like the apostles, Augustine, St. Francis, St. Patrick of Ireland, Luther, Wesley, Brainard, Judson, or Praying Hyde, we see such a gap between them and where we are. We become discouraged and do not begin to develop spiritual muscles in our prayer lives. But prayer is something that we can learn, and we can start where we are, and grow from where we are.

In the 1984 Olympic games in Los Angeles, we saw outstanding athletes like Carl Lewis, Mary Lou Retton, and Edwin Moses. Not one of these persons was "born" an Olympic champion. They began with nothing but desire and some natural ability, then worked for years and years to learn a discipline that finally brought strength and freedom into their lives. If this is true in athletics, which are of passing value, how much more discipline is needed to develop freedom and strength in our praying!

As I have studied Richard Foster's suggestions on prayer (and I confess that I feel so inadequate in this area that I have been through his book at least five times) I am intrigued by his methods. He tells of taking a copy of the New Testament and cutting out every reference to prayer in the Gospels. After pasting them onto sheets of paper, so he could read them at one time, he was shocked by what he saw. "Either the excuses and rationalizations for unanswered prayer I had been taught were wrong, or Jesus' words were wrong. I determined to learn to pray so that my experiences conformed to the words of Jesus rather than trying to make His words conform to my impoverished experience."[4]

Apart from my own discovery of prayer along these lines, I would never have become involved in the battle against obscenity, pornography, and the sexual revolution in America. Apart from these beginning lessons of discovering the greatness of God and the power of God, and the release of that power through prayer, I would have run from the battle. The battle is simply too great. Five months of meeting God each weekday at 6:30 A.M. for prayer gave birth to my involvement against pornography. Prayer is the power cell for action because prayer puts us in touch with God and His strength.

But during these years, it has continued to be a process, to quote Chuck Swindoll, "three steps forward and two steps back." I share this so that you will not be discouraged when the progress is not always constant and when the depth that you seek is not always found. In prayer we can take steps forward, and we can do much more; we can discover new energy and power for our lives and for our families, congregations, and denominations in which we serve, and for the communities and cities in which God has placed us.

I believe that God has allowed the pestilence of pornography in America to make us face the seriousness of our own sin, to break our hearts by revealing the desperate need for righteousness in our lives and in the church. Our own needs must drive us to the Lord and to each other at much deeper levels. God wants us to love as He loves. Through His eyes of love, He wants us to see the moral brokenness of people as He sees their brokenness. I believe we can learn to weep over the rebelliousness, selfishness, and lostness of our nation, to learn what it means to mourn.

> My eyes are spent with weeping;
>   my soul is in tumult;
> my heart is poured out in grief
>   because of the destruction
>   of the daughter of my
>   people (Lam. 2:11).

The people whom God loves and for whom Christ died, are lost, utterly destroyed, by sin. Jeremiah saw that lostness and wept over Israel and Judah. Jesus saw that lostness and wept over Jerusalem. The more we learn of God, and the closer we come to Him through prayer, the more deeply we feel the pain of sin—not only our own sin, but the pain of other sinners and the pain of the victim.

Abraham Heschel writes, "The prophet is a person who suffers the harms done to others. Wherever a crime is committed, it is as if the prophet were the victim and the prey...God is not indifferent to evil! He is always concerned, He is personally affected by what man does to man."[5] As Mother Teresa has urged us, we need to let our hearts be broken by the suffering that breaks the heart of God.

I think that I have experienced something like this kind of mourning on only two or three occasions in my life. And one of these occasions is what has prompted me to enter this struggle against the epidemic of pornography.

As I mentioned at the outset of this book, there is a hillside across the street from my home where I often go to be alone with God. As I was there before daybreak that one morning in early spring, I was contemplating the suffering of people in our country, and in my own congregation. I was thinking about the young people whose lives were being destroyed before they had a chance to live—women and men and little children—bruised and abused and discarded by the illicit sex industry. Finally, I could not stand the pain any longer. I cried out to God, "Why don't You do something about this?" Very seldom have I prayed that way, but I was hurt, angry, and desperate. It was something of a crisis of faith for me. I needed answers; I needed hope.

"God!" I exclaimed. "I know that You love these children, more than I can ever love them. How can You see them molested and not do something? I know that You love these women who are being violated and raped, and the men who have become so sexualized that they can't relate to women except as sex objects. Father! I know You love these persons whose marriages are broken and destroyed. I know You see the fear, the abuse, the violence, the perversion and slavery that is taking place. Surely You see it—why don't You do something about it?"

When I was finally so exhausted from my anguish and prayer that my own cries were silent, these words came quickly to my mind: "Jerry, why don't you do something about it?"

Some time passed in silence and awe.

Then these thoughts came to my mind: "You know that I love them, you know that I have chosen to love them through you, and through all My people. You do something about it. I will give you strength. I will guide your steps. But I won't do it apart from you. I will do it through you. I won't do for you what you can do, but I will do for you what you cannot do. Are you ready to let Me use you and My people?"

I do not know what I prayed after that, or how long I lingered on the hill. But I know that I was filled with awe, with exhilaration and thanksgiving. I was filled with hope.

What took place on that hillside? Was that a conversation with God? I didn't hear his voice; it took place within my heart. Was it my imagination and wishful thinking, or had God spoken to me? You must decide for yourself. As clearly as I can understand, God spoke to me, and the burden within me was lifted.

Has He spoken to you? Are you one of the army He is raising up for such a time as this?

I confess to you, I have not often wept over my own sins, much less the suffering and sins of others. But I can say that on the few occasions when tears have welled up from within me, I have experienced the blessedness Jesus describes when he promises, "Blessed are those who mourn, for they shall be comforted" (Matt. 5:4). I believe this is the kind of mourning and comfort that leads to new dimensions of prayer, and releases the power of the kingdom of God.

I need to go on and say that there has been a direct relationship between my health and my prayer, between my energy and my prayer, between my personal peace and my prayer, and between my fruitfulness and my prayer. I don't pray enough, I tend to do things through my own strength. If I don't pray enough, I tend to forget that the battle is the Lord's. I tend to own my problems rather than place them in God's hands and believe Him for the results.

TAPPING INTO THE POWER

There is a way of tapping into the power of God that has helped me catch a fresh vision of Him and of His power to fulfill His purpose and plan for creation. Taking one of the Epistles or a chapter or two of one of the Gospels, I study each paragraph, giving it a title. Then I memorize those titles so that I can think back through the context of that entire book or chapter at one sitting—out on the hill or under the stars, or in a traffic jam or check-out line at a discount store—or wherever I may be.

After memorizing the titles of the paragraphs, I memorize the text itself, so the Holy Scripture becomes part of my thinking process. As I fill my mind with the Word of God, and as I grow in believing what it says and standing on it, my prayers begin to be patterned by it. I find that I stop in the midst of reciting the text, and pray over those truths for individuals in my congregation, or a person across the country, and especially for the body of Christ. Prayer that squares with the Word of God is changing my prayer life.

At a very critical time for me, while memorizing the first chapter of Ephesians, I came to these verses:

> For he has made known to us in all wisdom and insight the mystery of his will, according to his purpose which he set forth in Christ as a plan for the fulness of time, to unite all things in him, things in heaven and things on earth. In him according to the purpose of him who accomplishes all things according to the counsel of his will, we who first hoped in Christ have been destined and appointed to live for the praise of his glory (vv. 9-12).

I realized in a totally new and personal way that God has a plan to unite through Christ all things in heaven and on earth, and that He plans to accomplish this through His people. He not only has a plan, but He has the power to fulfill that plan! Through another special time of prayer, I realized that God could and would bring together the denominational leaders across this country to tackle the problem of pornography. That realization—that sudden recognition of the power of God to unite the brethren through that particular Scripture—was the spark that burst into the flame that produced the National Consultation on Obscenity, Pornography, and Indecency and has become the National Coalition Against Pornography. The nationwide Christian community is uniting to war against the common enemy.

I agree with Richard Foster. After learning the promises of God and the teaching of the New Testament, I either must change the way I pray, or stop saying that Scripture is the inspired and authoritative Word of God. With Foster, I prefer to stand with Jesus and with God's promises of prayer rather than with my own limited experience. I am growing in prayer and I can say, "Lord, teach us to pray," and I mean it more than ever before.

Frank Laubach's book, *Prayer, the Mightiest Force in the World*, has helped me greatly, as has Hope Mac-Donald's, *Discovering How to Pray*, which contains practical steps for strengthening prayer. Paul Bilheimer's book, *Destined for the Throne*, is in a class of its own, dealing with the sovereignty of God and God's purpose in the world through the church.

And I am constantly encouraged by books and articles both by and about Mother Teresa, who expresses love of God so simply and so well: "The Lord never asks of us anything that he does not give us the power to do." [6] I believe that is true. And so I pray, "God, make me a man of prayer, and make your church a people of prayer. Lord, send renewal and awakening and revival to our home, and to your church."

SOME PRACTICAL STEPS

1. *Start where you are.* Take one step at a time. God loves us so much that He meets us right where we are, but He loves us too much to leave us where we are. Take one small but definite step in prayer and in faith today.

2. *Choose a specific place and time for prayer.* I usually eat breakfast and supper in the same place, and at almost the same time each day. I eat more regularly and healthfully that way. The same thing is true about prayer. If you choose the same place and use it daily, it becomes set apart as your special place of prayer.

3. *Choose the Scripture that has most encouraged you in prayer.* Pray those passages which have most strengthened you to do God's will in the past. Pray those truths for people you know. Pray that God will fulfill His promises and His plan for His kingdom and His glory. Pray that He will be honored.

4. *Keep a record of your requests and God's answers.* Allow God to strengthen your faith and release more fully within you a spirit of thanksgiving.

5. *Pray for moral and spiritual protection.* It's always important to seek divine protection from distractions, interruptions, and wandering thoughts that hinder concentration and growth in prayer. But more specifically, spiritual protection is crucial to our struggle against pornography. Sexual immorality is one of Satan's prime temptations. He's had virtually free rein for too long, and he's not about to give in without a fight. "For we are not contending against flesh and blood" (Eph. 6:12). Depression, sickness, discouragement, fear, rage, are all elements in the

spiritual warfare. As you enter into this battle, realize that you are entering into spiritual warfare.

The temptation of sexually explicit material itself is dangerous to men and women alike, and challenges our mental and spiritual well-being. Overestimating our resistance to sin is a constant hazard. Choose someone with whom you can be openly and regularly accountable to be your partner in prayer.

There are also those like Bruce Ritter and Morton Hill who are in direct hand-to-hand combat, as it were, with those who man the earthly outposts of the kingdom of darkness. They need prayer for bodily protection, and for spiritual protection as they literally put their lives on the line. Pray for Rev. Donald Wildmon, Brad Curl, Bruce Taylor, and Bill Swindell who are national leaders in the organized effort against obscenity. Pray for others you know who are entering this battle. "Units of prayer combined, like drops of water, make an ocean which defies resistance."[7] Organized crime knows no limit to protect its interest, but organized crime is no match for organized prayer.

INTERCESSION FOR THOSE WITH SEXUAL DEVIANCE

At College Hill Presbyterian Church, through the power of God released in prayer and counseling, consistent mutual accountability, and the continuing support of a compassionate community of believers, we have seen many persons with a variety of sexual deviances healed. We have seen homosexuals healed, pornography addicts transformed, pedophiles changed and persons caught in the web of incest saved. These persons have experienced God's grace and healing and have found a new freedom to live as God's children without fear and distrust. This ministry is rarely easy or painless; in fact, it is very often a long and painful process. But I want to say without any doubt that healing is possible, and prayer is the key.

Recently, I spoke with a man who was victimized by pornography during his childhood, and had led a promiscuous heterosexual lifestyle. He has had sexual relationships with literally hundreds of women. But he has been transformed by Jesus Christ and has been delivered from his promiscuous behavior. He is reunited with his wife, who has known God's healing power, not only for her marriage, but for the wounds of incest inflicted upon her during her childhood. These people were not healed overnight. But both husband and wife have been healed and are being renewed through the power of God through prayer.

Richard Foster writes:

> Sexual deviations can be prayed for with real assurance that a real and lasting change can occur. Sex is like a river—it is good and a wonderful blessing when kept within its proper channel. A river that overflows its banks is a dangerous thing, and so are perverted sexual drives. What are the God-created banks for sex? One man with one woman in a marriage for life. It is a joy, when praying for individuals with sexual problems, to visualize a river that has overflowed its banks and invite the Lord to bring it back into its natural channel.[8]

Prayer is the first tool, the strong foundation on which we stand, and the starting place from which we can march out with power against the forces of pornography, obscenity, and indecency. But prayer is not the only tool, and the foundation is not the finish. We must equip ourselves with all the tools necessary to do the job and do it right.

ENDNOTES

1. Catherine Marshall, *Adventure in Prayer* (New York: Ballantine, 1980), 19-27.

2. Richard Foster, *Celebration of Discipline*, (San Francisco: Harper and Row, 1978), 1.

3. Ibid., 30.

4. Ibid., 33.

5. Abraham J. Heschel, *The Prophets*, vol. 2. (New York: Harper and Row, 1962), 65.

6. See the bibliography for these and other helpful materials.

7. E.M. Bounds, *Power Through Prayer* (Grand Rapids: Baker, 1972), 83.

8. Foster, 38.

For more information about this area of healing and the church as a therapeutic community, write The Teleios Center, College Hill Presbyterian Church, 5742 Hamilton Avenue, Cincinnati, Ohio 45224.

Chapter 7

Our Greatest Earthly Ally

The protection given speech and press was fashioned to assure unfettered interchange of ideas for the bringing about of political and social changes desired by the people.
Roth, 354, U.S. at 484

The dissenting justices sound the alarm of repression. But in our view, to equate the free and robust exchange of ideas and political debate with commercial exploitation of obscene material demeans the grand conception of the First Amendment and its high purposes in the historic struggle for freedom.
Chief Justice Berger, *Miller*, 413 U.S. at 34

Pornography must be legal, people think to themselves. *There must be nothing wrong with it because the government allows it to exist.*

Wrong! Pornography, particularly hard-core pornography, is illegal.

To fight effectively against pornography, you and I need to know that we have an incredibly strong ally: the laws of our nation. The laws are being flagrantly violated by pornographers, but even our concerned citizens are allowing the violations to persist because they are unaware of the power of already existing laws and they fail to demand enforcement.

Many people feel unqualified to talk about enforcement to the media, city prosecutors, and others who have legal knowledge. Some have bought a line of thinking that has been propagated by the propornography folks. I call it the "First Amendment lie"— the erroneous presupposition that obscenity is protected by the "freedom of speech" clause of the U.S. Constitution.

By becoming familiar with the material in this chapter, you will have a solid foundation on which to use the law as a powerful ally. You will have strong, accurate answers for the vast majority of those who would raise legal smokescreens.[1]

WHAT LAWS EXIST

A series of federal laws give protection against pornography. These are briefly outlined below:

Adult Pornography	1. if imported—felony.[2]
	2. if transported—interstate felony[3]
	3. if mailed—felony[4]
	4. if transported by common carrier (U.P.S., bus, taxi, etc.)—felony[5]
Child Pornography	(depicting age seventeen or under)
	5. if commercial (for sale) or private use—felony, enacted May 1984[6]
Both Adult and Child Pornography	6. if words or pictures broadcast via radio communication (radio, cable, and noncable TV)—felony[7]

7. R.I.C.O. obscenity—(discussed in Chapter 3) included in the Federal Racketeer-Influenced and Corrupt Organization Act as of October 1984[8]

Besides the federal statutes, all states, with the exception of Alaska, have laws against pornography. Many have specific laws that prohibit the sale of materials harmful to minors which includes pornographic material. Many communities have local ordinances to control particular aspects of the sale or distribution of pornography. For example, the city of Cincinnati negotiated a contract for cable television services that has prohibited the showing of X-rated materials. The city or county prosecutors in your area can tell you what state and local laws exist; or you can seek assistance from Citizens for Decency through Law, or from Morality in Media.

WINNING THROUGH INTIMIDATION

If the laws exist, why don't more people press for enforcement? In many cases, propornography advocates have "won" battles by using the tactic of intimidation. They ask legal questions that require lengthy answers and make intimidating remarks to those who challenge them. Unfortunately, these clichés are often picked up by the media. They need to be recognized for what they are: smokescreens to divert attention from the clarity of the law. Three of the most common clichés are:

• The Supreme Court has never defined pornogra-

phy or obscenity adequately. One person's pornography is another person's poetry.
- Freedom of expression is guaranteed by the
  First Amendment.
- Morality can't be legislated. Who are you to tell
  me what I can see or read? You don't have to
  look at the films or the books. Don't interfere
  with my right to do what I want. Stop imposing
  your morality on me!

Make no mistake, these are not casual statements.
They are carefully framed to cast doubts in the minds
of not only the general public, but those in the legal
community as well. It is from the legal profession
that the most outspoken critics of laws to regulate
pornography have arisen. These critics have labored
long and hard to convince anyone who would listen
that obscenity and pornography are such vague concepts they cannot be adequately defined. Moreover, it
is these same critics who have championed the unten-
able position that obscenity and pornography are
speech protected by the First Amendment, and that
such material merely involves aspects of private morality which should not be subject to regulation.

The United States Supreme Court has categorically, uniformly, and repeatedly rejected these rationalizations. But these positions persist, in part
because a minority of justices on the Supreme Court
have supported these positions, and in part because
people in the media who agree with this minority position use their platforms to express and defend their
convictions. To add to the problem, those members of
the legal profession who have advocated tough obscenity and pornography law enforcement have often

failed to explain with care the extent of protection the law affords. They need to focus the definition of obscenity correctly so that it is clear and does not impinge on authentic First Amendment rights.

How then are the critics wrong?

TWO LEGAL OBJECTIONS

There are two major legal objections given in an effort to halt obscenity and pornography legislation, both of which appeal to the Constitution.

The first objection is based on the "due process" clause of the Fourteenth Amendment. No state shall "deprive any person of life, liberty, or property, without due process of law."[9] This clause has been interpreted to mean that all criminal statutes must provide reasonably understandable standards so that people know what is and is not against the law. If a statute is so vague that an adequate notice of illegal conduct is not given, the law is considered null and void.

The Supreme Court landmark decision in *Miller vs. California* upheld the constitutionality of obscenity laws and set forth the court's most recent definition of obscenity, which I will discuss a few paragraphs later. One of the dissenting justices argued that *obscenity* was so incapable of definition that laws using the term were "void for vagueness."[10] The other three dissenting justices in *Miller* adopted this same position in *Paris Adult Theater vs. Slaton*."[11]

The second objection is based on the "freedom of speech" clause in the First Amendment. This clause provides that "Congress shall make no law...abridging freedom of speech, or the press."[12] Two former justices of the Supreme Court (William O. Douglas and Hugo Black) steadfastly argued that obscenity was "speech" protected by the First Amendment, and therefore not subject to censorship.[13]

OBSCENITY AND PORNOGRAPHY DEFINED

Before either of the preceding points can be satisfactorily addressed, obscenity and pornography must be defined. Once the clear and concise legal definitions of *obscenity* and *pornography* are understood, most of the critics' objections disappear. The issue, by the way, is not how you or I define obscenity, but rather, how the Supreme Court defines obscenity.

The word *obscene* is derived from the Latin word *obscaenus* (*ob*, meaning "to," and *caenum*, meaning "filth"). *Obscenity* is commonly used to refer to things that are considered disgusting, foul, repulsive, or filthy. In addition, *obscenity* denotes that which is offensive to modesty or common decency.

When the law uses the term *obscenity*, however, it takes on a narrower and more specific meaning. In *Miller*, the Supreme Court set forth a three-part test to define what it meant by the term *obscenity*. The basic guidelines must be:

a. Whether the average person, applying contemporary community standards would find that the work, taken as a whole, appeals to the prurient interest;

b. whether the work depicts or describes, in a patently offensive way, sexual conduct specifically defined by the applicable state law; and

c. whether the work taken as a whole, lacks serious literary, artistic, political, or scientific value.[14]

Although the Supreme Court's test for obscenity

might appear somewhat cryptic at first glance, its meaning is really quite simple. In defining obscenity the high court has attempted to identify what is commonly referred to as hard-core pornography.[15]

Recall that pornography is usually defined as writings or pictures intended to arouse sexual desire. Hard-core pornography is limited to the explicit description or depiction of ultimate sexual acts, such as intercourse, masturbation, oral sex, or to the lewd exhibition of the genitals.[16] Thus, obscenity refers to graphic depictions or descriptions of sexual activity that are calculated to cause sexual arousal in the reader or viewer. *Obscenity is nothing more than a means whereby one is titillated or sexually stimulated.* The point of obscenity is to facilitate sexual activity and nothing more.

THE SUPREME COURT'S THREE-PART TEST

Although it isn't necessary to go through an exhaustive analysis of the Supreme Court's test, it is important to touch on each of the three areas and explain how each one is related to defining hard-core pornography.

The focus of the first point is on "prurient interest." This simply means material that produces sexual stimulation, the well-known biological and physical response. This, therefore, prevents obscenity's being confused with valid instructive material which serves to describe, discuss, or advocate human sexuality.[17] Is the material in question designed to *teach*, or is it meant to *turn on* the reader and/or viewer?

The focus of the second point is on "patent offensiveness." It appears that the court adopted this standard to identify only the most explicit and graphic pornography; that is, hard-core pornography. If the material depicts or describes ultimate sexual acts or lewd exhibition of the genitals, it can be considered patently offensive.[18] Pictures involving sado-masochistic sexual activities or pictures of penile erection in scenes suggesting that penetration or oral sex is imminent are also proscribed.

The final part of the tripartite test focuses on whether the work has serious literary, artistic, political, or scientific value. Its purpose is to exclude from obscenity depictions or descriptions of sex which may incidentally be sexually arousing, but that have another bona fide purpose. For example, a medical book for the education of doctors may have a very explicit depiction or description of sexual conduct. Some individuals might find this material arousing, but because it has a scientific purpose or application, outside of and unrelated to its possible titillating effect, it would not be considered obscene.

THE VAGUENESS PROBLEM

The critics claim that this three-part test is so vague that no one really knows what material can be considered obscene. Their position is simply false. Both the purveyor of pornography and the buyer of pornography know exactly what it is. The pornographer knows his business; his material is intended to be sexually arousing. The names of the magazines, books, and movies, as well as the advertisements for such material, belie any claim that the pornographer is ignorant of the trade he practices. Moreover, the product consists of material that can only be explained by the fact that the pornographer is aware of what "turns people on."

If you were to visit X-rated bookstores in New York, Chicago, and Los Angeles, you would find substantially the same material. In fact, anyone familiar with pornography could describe in detail what material would be found in any "adult entertainment" store in the country. The reason this is possible is because there is no more mystery about what pornography is than there is a mystery about what sex is.

Does the pornographer know this material violates the patent offensiveness rule? Again, this standard identifies depictions or descriptions of ultimate sexual acts or lewd exhibition of the genitals. Doesn't the pornographer know what an ultimate sexual act is and when his works depict or describe such acts as a means of sexual arousal? Of course he does.

Finally, the pornographer knows when his material lacks serious literary, artistic, political, or scientific value. No one, much less the pornographer, will be apt to confuse an explicit depiction of lesbians having oral sex in *Penthouse* with the descriptions of sex in a biology or medical textbook. Sex in the Bible or in Shakespeare is certainly not akin to the pornography market. To be sure, pornographers often contend that they cannot distinguish their pornography from classic works of science, literature, and art. But if this is so, why is it that pornographers never stock those classical works, Bibles, or medical texts?

Once again, pornographers are interested in providing their clientele with sex; literature, art, politics, and science are the furthest things from their minds. After all, if pornographers interjected serious literary value in their material, it would detract from its erotic appeal.

The Supreme Court has repeatedly held that the definition of obscenity is clear and understandable enough to overcome any "due process" or "vagueness" issues. Even though the Court has recognized that there is some imprecision in the definition of obscenity, it has consistently held that this "lack of precision is not itself offensive to the requirements of due process."[19] The " 'Constitution does not require impossible standards'; all that is required is that the language 'conveys sufficiently definite warning as to the proscribed conduct when measured by common understanding and practices.' "[20]

The tripartite test for judging obscenity already discussed gives adequate warning of the conduct proscribed. Further, it marks " 'boundaries sufficiently distinct for judges and juries fairly to administer the law....That there may be marginal cases in which it is difficult to determine the side of the line on which a particular situation falls is not sufficient reason to hold the language too ambiguous to define a criminal offense.' "[21]

The moment a publisher or producer deals in material that is calculated to arouse sexual desire by depicting or describing ultimate sexual acts, he has crossed over the line of demarcation into the zone of illegality. And pornographers know when they have crossed the line. They do it by design. In fact, their intention is to move continuously far beyond the line because stronger material is constantly needed to satisfy the prurient needs of the clientele.

Critics of pornography legislation within the legal

profession are markedly inconsistent. While some display an unusual sensitivity to the alleged imprecision they see in the definition of obscenity, they seldom criticize the imprecision found in other terms widely used in criminal law.

For example, the term *negligence* is used in the criminal laws of every state. Almost every crime requires some conscious wrongdoing. In some instances the requirement of guilty intention is fulfilled if the individual acted negligently. Negligence is the failure to exercise that degree of care which the ordinary "reasonable" individual would have exercised in the same situation. Such a standard is obviously imprecise and somewhat vague. Some states require the negligence to be "wanton" or "flagrant," which simply makes the issue more vague. Even the Constitution uses the terms "unreasonable searches and seizures," but what is "unreasonable"? "Unfair trade practices" are outlawed, but what is "unfair"? And the Sherman Act forbids "attempts to monopolize." What are "attempts"?

All of this highlights the fact that obscenity, when compared to other terms used and accepted in the criminal law, is at least as understandable and definable. When critics of legal standards to guard against obscenity stridently attack such legislation on "due process" grounds, their emotional fervor does more to reveal their underlying bias against prohibiting the sale of obscenity than it does to reveal their sincere concern with adequate definitions.

The same bias and inconsistency also show up when the pro-pornography forces are apparently willing to protect unconsenting adults and children from obscenity. Many porn advocates favor subjecting obscenity to zoning ordinances and nuisance laws. But if obscenity cannot be adequately defined to prohibit its sale to consenting adults, how can it be adequately defined under a law to protect unconsenting adults and children? By advocating protection for unconsenting adults and children, they have unwittingly conceded that *obscenity can be defined!*

While the current law clearly does permit effective action to be taken, Miller vs. California contains phraseology that often has been exploited to wriggle free from the law. This is why our job would be greatly facilitated if legislation were enacted forbidding the distribution through interstate commerce, "whether by printed material or filmed material, by air waves or by wireless communication, of any *visual* portrayal of ultimate sexual acts for purposes of commercial entertainment."

Such a law would eliminate, once and for all, lingering charges of vagueness, would remove the danger that "book burning" or "book banning" charges would cripple our cause, and would promote more expeditious and effective law enforcement. Such a law would drive pornography underground—where it was twenty-five years ago.

Would the Supreme Court accept such a law? No one knows for sure but the Court is heading in a more conservative direction.

THE FIRST AMENDMENT: IS OBSCENITY PROTECTED SPEECH?

Given that the current definition of obscenity and pornography is workable, some individuals would still go on to assert that obscene and pornographic material is protected speech under the First Amendment. The Supreme Court has never agreed with that proposition, but has stated: "This much has been categorically settled by the court, that obscene material is unprotected by the First Amendment."[22]

In the Supreme Court's landmark decision in *Roth vs. United States*, two reasons were given for excluding obscenity from the protection of the First Amendment.

First, the Court found that the First Amendment's concept of free speech was never absolute.[23]

When the Constitution was ratified, many types of speech, such as libel, blasphemy, or profanity were already state crimes. In 1712, Massachusetts made it a criminal act to publish anything obscene. Although the Court recognized that obscenity law was not well developed when the Constitution was written and ratified, the majority noted that case law early in the 1800s recognized the concept of obscenity. Statutory law dealing with obscenity became common during the first half of the nineteenth century.[24] From this historical perspective, the Court concluded that those responsible for our Constitution *never* intended to protect obscenity when they chose to protect speech.[25]

Those who argue the Constitution protects obscene material must realize they are forcing their own personal views upon the rest of the American people—in a most undemocratic manner. Ironically the critics of obscenity law turn the tables and charge those who favor such laws with imposing their will on the majority! This is one of the most flagrant lies surrounding the issue.

Obscenity laws have been duly passed by democratic legislatures throughout the entire history of our nation. At no time in the United States' history would two-thirds of the members of Congress and three-fourths of the states have passed an amendment to our Constitution protecting commercial traffic in obscenity and pornography.

It is the opponents of obscenity laws who want to short-circuit the will of the majority and the democratic process. They want the Supreme Court to overturn laws passed by almost every state. In the case of obscenity, the Supreme Court has done precisely the opposite. It has not only refused to overturn the existing state laws, it has defended and supported those laws.

Second, the Court has held that obscenity is not protected by the First Amendment because it has no expressive value or function. Obscenity simply is not speech.

The court explained: "[the] protection given speech and press was fashioned to assure unfettered interchange of ideas for the bringing about of political and social changes desired by the people."[26] Instead, the Court took the position that because obscenity had nothing to do with the unfettered interchange of ideas, it could not be considered speech.

More recently, the Supreme Court has echoed that sentiment: "But, in our view, to equate the free and robust exchange of ideas and political debate with commercial exploitation of obscene material demeans the grand conception of the First Amendment and its high purposes in the historic struggle for freedom."[27]

One scholar who has supported the Supreme Court's obscenity decisions is John M. Finnis, a fellow of University College, Oxford. Dr. Finnis argues that speech pertains to the realm of ideas, reason, intellectual content, and truth seeking. Obscenity is not speech because it pertains to the realm of passion, desires, cravings, and titillation.[28] Dr. Finnis may have framed the issues best when he wrote: "The fundamental question is simple: does the reader look for 'titillation' or for 'intellectual content'? "[29] Because obscenity and pornography contain no intellectual content, such material cannot be considered speech.

IF NOT SPEECH, WHAT?

This same point has also been forcefully stated by a leading legal commentator. Professor Frederick Schauer of the Marshall-Wythe School of Law, College of William and Mary, has argued that the essence of speech under the First Amendment is intellectual communication.[30] Speech has cognitive content; it appeals to our minds and enhances knowledge.

Obscenity is not involved in the communication of intellectual concepts; it is not even a proposition about sex or an argument for sex. Obscenity is the portrayal of sexual conduct for purposes of arousal. Professor Schauer explains:

> The key to understanding the court's treatment of pornography as nonspeech is the realization that the *primary purpose of pornography is to produce sexual excitement*. The distinction between the pornographic and the sexually explicit is completely artificial unless pornography is viewed as essentially a physical rather than a mental stimulus.
>
> Thus the refusal to treat pornography as speech is grounded in the assumption that the prototypical pornographic item on closer analysis *shares more of the*

characteristics of sexual activity than of the communicative process. The pornographic item is in a real sense a sexual surrogate. It takes pictorial or linguistic form only because some individuals achieve sexual gratification by those means.[31]

Professor Schauer's explanation is consistent with the research of Doctors Dietz and Evans cited in Chapter 2.

Interestingly, Justices Black and Douglas, the two Supreme Court members who argued that obscenity is protected speech, did so because they saw it as valid speech. They repeatedly referred to obscenity as "discussion," "opinion," "idea," "thought," or "view" about sex.[32] On one occasion Justice Douglas even implied that obscenity was an idea "competing for acceptance."[33] There is at least one possible explanation for Justice Douglas' stance. He indicated that *he had never viewed obscene material including the material which came before the court.*[34]

"IF YOU DON'T LIKE IT, DON'T BUY IT"

"If you don't like porn films or books, you don't have to see them or buy them. But don't interfere with my rights to see or buy them." Ever hear that argument? Sounds free and noble at first, doesn't it? But the Supreme Court has spoken clearly to this issue, concluding that there are significant reasons for maintaining laws regulating or prohibiting commerce in obscenity.

Take for example, the *Paris Adult Theater vs. Slaton* decision: The court noted that a free market for obscene material had a tendency to affect adversely our quality of life, the total community environment, and the tone of commerce in our cities.[35] To quote Professor Alexander Bickel of Yale Law School, a former law clerk to Justice Felix Frankfurter:

> It concerns the tone of the society, the mode, or to use terms that have perhaps greater currency, the style and quality of life, now and in the future. A man may be entitled to read an obscene book in his room, or expose himself indecently there....We should protect his privacy. But if he demands a right to obtain the books and pictures he wants in the market, and to foregather in public places—discreet, if you will, but accessible to all—with others who share his tastes then to grant him his right is to affect the world about the rest of us, and to impinge on other privacies. Even supposing that each of us can, if he wishes, effectively avert the eye and stop the ear (which, in truth, we cannot), what is commonly read and seen and heard and done intrudes upon us all, want it or not.[36]

A number of years ago Lord Devlin, a renowned British jurist, made the same point, and his arguments were reviewed by Ronald Dworkin, also of Yale Law School:

> If we permit obscene books freely to be sold, to be delivered as it were the morning milk, the whole tone of the community will eventually change....A public which could enjoy pornography legally would soon settle for nothing much tamer, and all forms of popular culture would inevitably move closer to the salacious.[37]

Professor Dworkin also points out that social practices are corrupted through forces beyond our control. At some point the majority would not object to further deterioration of community standards, but that was a sign of the corruption's success, "not proof that there has been no corruption" at all.[38] His conclusion was that it is "precisely that possibility which makes it imperative that we enforce our standards while we still have them."[39]

The Supreme Court also pointed out that there was an arguable correlation between obscenity and crime.[40] The critics of obscenity laws can no longer dismiss the very real possibility that hard-core pornography, and in particular pornography mixed with violence, contributes to and leads to antisocial behavior. The majority conclusion of the President's Commission on Obscenity and Pornography of 1970, that there was no evidence of harmful effects stemming from the use of such material, was soundly repudiated by the Senate at that time, as well as by the "Hill-Link" Minority Report. The majority conclusion of that commission has since been clearly contradicted by a burgeoning body of independent research.

There is also mounting evidence of long-term harmful effects that can be attributed to an easing of sexual norms. Many researchers and numerous historians have indicated that civilization itself may ultimately be threatened by permissive sexual standards.[41]

At this point in the discussion the critics of obscenity legislation almost always observe that harmful effects stemming from obscenity are not conclusively established. This, of course, is true. No one can prove that reading one specific magazine caused one specific man to commit one specific crime.

But few matters are established with scientific certainty. Accordingly, the court has rejected the notion that it is not possible to regulate obscenity as long as conclusive proof of its adverse effects was lacking. The court concluded that legislatures were not required to have "scientifically certain criteria" before they acted.[42] Indeed, legislatures, as well as judges, juries, presidents, and administrative agencies, seldom if ever have absolute proof before they act.

The court also disposed of the assertion that individuals have a "right of privacy" protecting market transactions in obscenity.[43] This argument gained appeal when the Supreme Court in *Stanley vs. Georgia* held that states could not make the possession of obscenity in one's home a crime.[44] Based on that premise, it has been argued that one should have a right to acquire obscene material. (After all, what sense is there in giving a person a constitutional right to possess obscenity if there is not a right to purchase or acquire the material?)

The court, however, ruled that the right to be free from criminal prosecution for private possession of obscenity stems, not from an absolute right to procure or possess the material, but from a right to have personal intimacies in one's home secured.[45] Accordingly, the court stressed there is no right to display obscenity in public places or to distribute it in the marketplace.[46]

Finally, the court categorically rejected the proposition that conduct involving consenting adults should not be subject to state regulation.[47] Anglo-American law has never accepted this proposition. Numerous laws affect consenting adults: labor laws, antitrust laws, drug abuse laws, laws against prostitution, suicide, voluntary self-mutilation, bare fist fights, and duels, to name only a few.

Another type of law analogous to our obscenity laws are laws against dog fights and cock fights. One reason for those laws, of course, is to protect animals. But their primary reason is to secure the humanity of our fellows. Our legislators felt men and women were debased and degraded by being entertained at the sight of dogs and roosters tearing each other to death. How much more is humanity debased and counteredified by viewing rape of women or children for "entertainment value"?

Pornography teaches us that sex is a recreational activity without deeper meaning. Gone from sex is love, commitment, and affection. Instead, sex is a game and the participants are toys to be used and abused for a few moments' fun and entertainment. And it does not matter what form the sexual activity takes as long as sexual excitement and satisfaction are achieved.

Accordingly, it is not uncommon to find pornography that invites the viewer to participate in bizarre forms of sex, like necrophilia (sex with dead people), bestiality (sex with animals), homosexuality (sex with members of the same sex), sadomasochism (sex involving torture) and pedophilia (sex with children). Some pornographers also pander to scatological interests. Believe it or not, some persons are apparently attracted to sex involving excretory functions and this category of pornography has grown rapidly in recent years.

Rape is another favorite theme of the pornographers. As we have discussed, many men are excited by violent sexual assaults on women, particularly if the woman is ultimately shown to be enjoying the assault.

The Mind Polluters

The misuse and perversion of sex has had a terribly adverse impact upon our society. It has contributed to an epidemic of venereal disease, unwanted pregnancies, abortions, divorces, broken families, and sexual child abuse. There is no question that our society has a vital interest in promoting conduct which works toward the dignity of all people. Although it cannot be said that the sale of obscenity "directly and immediately" causes all of these evils, common sense indicates that its sale makes the abuse of sex more likely. The following conclusion of the Supreme Court is certainly warranted:

> The sum of experience, including that of the past two decades, affords ample basis for legislatures to conclude that a sensitive, key relationship of human existence, central to family life, community welfare, and the development of human personality, can be debased and distorted by crass commercial exploitation of sex. Nothing in the Constitution prohibits a state from reaching such a conclusion and acting on it legislatively....[48]

Obscenity is Illegal!

ENDNOTES

1. Since I am not a legal authority, Tom Grossmann, a Christian lawyer who is part of our Cincinnati team, collaborated with me in writing this chapter. The content of this chapter has been verified by Dr. Paul McGeady of the National Obscenity Law Center, one of the leading authorities on obscenity law in the country. It has also been reviewed and substantiated by Mr. Bruce Taylor, executive vice president of Citizens for Decency Through Law, who has personally led in over three thousand obscenity court cases and is Senior Legal Advisor to this outstanding national organization.
2. 18 U.S.C. section 1462.
3. Ibid.
4. 18 U.S.C. section 1461.

5. 18 U.S.C. section 1462.

6. 18 U.S.C. sections 2251-2253.

7. 18 U.S.C. section 1464.

8. 18 U.S.C. section 1961.

9. U.S. Constitution amendment XIV.

10. 413 U.S. 15, 37 (1973) (Douglas, J., dissenting).

11. 413 U.S. 49, 73 (1973) (Brennan, J., dissenting, joined by Stewart, J., and Marshall, J.).

12. U.S. Constitution amendment I.

13. E.g., *Roth vs. United States*, 354 U.S. 476, 508 (1957) (Douglas, J., dissenting, joined by Black, J.).

14. 413 U.S., 24.

15. Ibid., 27-29.

16. Ibid., 25.

17. *See* Schauer, Speech and "Speech"—Obscenity and "Obscenity": An Exercise in the Interpretation of Constitutional Language, 67 *Georgetown Law Journal* 899, 928 (1979) ["The concept fundamental to the *Miller* test is that material appealing to the prurient interest *is* sex, and not merely describing or advocating sex. Material that appeals to the prurient interest is material that turns you on. Period."]

In *Roth vs. United States*, 354 U.S., 476, 487 n. 20 (1957), the court defined prurient interest as "Material having a tendency to excite lustful thoughts." The court also went on to quote the definition of prurient interest found in the Model Penal Code; "a shameful or morbid interest in nudity, sex, or excretion...." *Id.* This later definition should not be cause for confusion. It is evident from numerous Supreme Court cases that the "prurient interest" test for obscenity is meant to identify erotic material, even though this material may also be shameful or morbid. E.g., *Miller*, 413 U.S., 18-19 n. 2 (1973) [The court explained that obscenity referred to pornography, or material "designed to cause sexual excitement."]; *Ginzburg vs. United States*, 383 U.S., 463, 470-71 (1966) [The court declared that the material could be found obscene because the "titillating," "erotically arousing," and sexually stimulating aspects of the material were stressed to the exclusion of all other aspects.]

18. *Jenkins vs. Georgia*, 418 U.S., 153 (1974).

19. E.g., *Roth vs. United States*, 354 U.S., 476, 491 (1957).

20. Ibid., (quoting *United States vs. Petrilla*, 332 U.S., 1, 7-8).

21. Ibid., 491-92. See also *Miller*, 413 U.S., 27 n. 10.

22. *Miller*, 413 U.S., 23.

23. 354 U.S., 482.

24. Ibid., 482-83.

25. Ibid., 483.

26. Ibid., 484.

27. *Miller*, 413 U.S., 34.

28. John M. Finnis, "Reason and Passion": The Constitutional Dialectic of Free Speech and Obscenity, 116 *University of Pennsylvania Law Review* 222 (1967).

29. Ibid., 240.

30. Schauer, supra note 17.

The Mind Polluters

31. Ibid., 922-23. Emphasis added.

32. E.g., *Miller*, 413 U.S., 44-47 (Douglas, J., dissenting); *Ginzburg vs. United States*, 383 U.S., 463, 476 and 482 (dissenting opinions of Black, J., and Douglas, J.).

33. *Miller*, 413 U.S., 47.

34. *Paris Adult Theater*, 413 U.S., at 71 (Douglas, J., dissenting).

35. Ibid., 57-59.

36. Ibid., 59.

37. Dworkin, *Lord Devlin and the Enforcement of Morals*, 75 Yale *Law Journal*, 986, 1003 (1966).

38. Ibid., 1004.

39. Ibid.

40. Paris Adult Theater, 413 U. S. at 58 and N. 8.

41. Dr. Reo M. Christenson of Miami University (Ohio) has collected some of this evidence in his book, *Challenge and Decision: Political Issues of Our Time* (5th ed. 1976), p. 209.

[S]tudents of behavior are remarkably united in their view that declining sexual standards lead to a deteriorating society. Cambridge scholar J.D. Unwin, surveying the sexual practices of eighty primitive and many more advanced societies, concluded that sexually permissive behavior led to less cultural energy, creativity, individualism, and a slower movement toward advanced civilization: "...throughout the world and throughout history, a greater or lesser mental development has accompanied a limitation or extension of sexual opportunity."

Unwin says there is no known instance of a society that retained as high a cultural level after relatively permissive sexual standards replaced more rigorous ones. (He conceded that it might take several generations before the debilitating effect was fully manifested.) Unwin arrived at his views, interestingly, through intensive anthropological research which he had hoped would disprove the thesis he finally accepted.

William Stephens, after studying ninety cultures, wrote that the tribes lowest on the scale of cultural evolution have the most sexual freedom. (Those with "maximal freedom" show "little connection between sex and love," he also states.)

Harvard sociologist Pitirim Sorokin's extensive studies convinced him that societies that disapprove of sex outside of marriage "provide an environment more favorable for creative growth" than those that do not. Sorokin concedes that the relaxation of unusually severe and prolonged sexual repression may be accompanied by a temporary increase in a group's creativity. But if permissive sexual standards continue, creativity soon declines. Arnold J. Toynbee, the most celebrated student of world civilizations, asserts that a culture that postpones rather than stimulates sexual experiences in young adults is a culture most prone to progress.

42. *Paris Adult Theater*, 413 U.S., 60-61.
43. Ibid., 65.
44. 394 U.S., 557 (1969).
45. *Paris Adult Theater*, 413 U.S., 65.
46. Ibid., 65-66.
47. Ibid., 68-69.
48. Ibid., 63.

Chapter 8

The Nature of a Movement

The most radical social teaching of Jesus was His total reversal of the contemporary notion of greatness. Leadership is found in becoming the servant of all. Power is discovered in submission. The foremost symbol of this radical servanthood is the cross. "He [Jesus] humbled himself and became obedient unto death, even death on a cross" (Phil. 2:8). But note this: Christ not only died a cross-death, He lived a cross-life. The way of the cross, the way of a suffering servant, was essential to His ministry. Jesus lived the cross-life in submission to His fellow human beings. He was the servant of all.

Richard Foster, *Celebration of Discipline*, 101

Fire produces two forms of energy: heat and light. Both can be useful when harnessed and directed, but both can be destructive: light can either illuminate or blind; heat can either save or destroy.

Recognizing that the evil of pornography can put the fire of anger into your bones, anger can also impel you to take action. Yet anger without the light that comes from knowledge of God can become fanaticism, and the last thing we need is to deserve the label "fanatics."

But light without heat can be ineffective. We can study every book available about pornography, and weep a million tears, but until we are motivated enough to *do* something, nothing will be changed. We need a balance of light and heat, knowledge behind intense motivation and action. We want a team of committed persons who really have the light of knowledge beneath the heat of their enthusiasm.

In the war against pornography, we need an army, a movement, that acts out of an awareness of the facts, not out of desperation or anger. The time and effort to gain effective knowledge in all areas is costly, but I'm asking you to make that sacrifice, because it will create the power we need to win this battle. We must approach others calmly, rationally, and confidently.

THE LONE RANGER

An independent leader has immediate strengths but in the long haul will never build a sense of momentum. The Lone Ranger will attract people, to be sure, who are moved by his courage and admire his style. But only those who are willing to stand in his shadow, like Tonto, stick around for any length of time. The Lone Ranger is looking for admirers, a clientele who will support his specific agenda, people of lesser ability or those whose gifts have not yet matured. But rather than building a team, or committing himself to other leaders, the Lone Ranger is busy watching for another sunset into which he can ride.

In taking on the pornography crowd, we are taking on a movement. There is camaraderie, common goals, mutual defense. A voice here, a protest there, will not cut it. We must face a movement *with* a movement.

The media loves to find one person who seems to be leading the way, and then make that leader a fool. No matter how strong the leader is, if the press decides that they want to expose his blind side, reveal her weaknesses and warts, it can do a thorough job. That's one of the great weaknesses of a "Lone Ranger." He or she is a lightning rod for investigative reporters!

A more significant weakness is that no one has a corner on wisdom. We need insight from each other for balance and perspective. The stronger the leader, the more important it is that he or she have many counselors and take their input seriously. The one in charge must also be under authority.

The biblical concept of the body of Christ stands in contrast to the Lone Ranger style. The body of Christ functions organically, demonstrating the partnership in ministry concept. This principle is not manipulation or a technique to get people motivated. Partnership in ministry means that the ministry is actually given to clergy and laity together. Leadership teams replace the concept of individual leaders and followers, enabling each member to release their abilities toward a common goal.

M-RIVETS

One of our strategies is to build a team by shared leadership that is so prepared and sizable, with a knowledge base and a style that is Christian, consistent with our stated commitment, that when the press or media challenge us, we can respond with knowledge and sensitivity and not appear foolish.

The "M-rivet" concept is a handy tool for understanding the principles of mobilization and how it functions through servant leadership.

M stands for *mobilizer*. Everyone, to one degree or another, has the gift of mobilizing others. For some, the size of group they can mobilize is small; for others, it is almost limitless. Those leaders who possess this gift need to use it to train others to exercise this gift as well. A strong team will not be built without it. A servant leader does not have to be the mobilizer but does need to see to it that this gift is released continually.

R—recruiter. Mobilizing starts with recruiting and enlarging the team. This is someone who believes strongly enough in the vision to be able to call others to commitment to a common goal and is willing to ask them to join the team, to come to the learning sessions and to give their energy to help define and accomplish the task.

I—inspirer. Mobilizing with staying power builds on inspiration. We are inspired by God and by the task, but we are also inspired by the love, encouragement, and commitment of those around us. Every group needs a self-starter. Every group needs persons who nurture and lift up others. Inspiration comes from worship, prayer, and growing obedience to the Lord and fellowship with one another.

*V—imparting *vision*. The mobilizer is usually able to recruit and inspire because he or she has a vision that has gripped and changed his life. This is the person who gives clarity to the direction and goal—seeing what needs to be done and what can be done through us, working together.

E—equipping others. Paul talks of persons gifted "to equip the saints for the work of ministry" (Eph. 4:12). The Greek word means literally, "mending the fishing nets," so they will be whole and able to handle the catch. Equipping is the process by which persons become more whole in the grace of God. It is the mending of our lives through teaching and worship so that we can give ourselves to the battle—in this case, the battle against pornography. Equipping is the process of multiplication by which we reproduce in others the light and the heat; the knowledge and the commitment that will ultimately lead to influence and victory.

T—trusting those who are equipped. It is believing that God has called them to share in this movement; believing that their gifts are important, that their ideas are important, that their contribution is important. If we believe in them, they will believe in themselves. If we believe that God will work through them, they will believe that God will use them. This multiplies leadership through the M-rivet concept.

Each person has the potential of being an M-rivet, or at least to begin the process, if only in the sense of recruiting and inspiring someone else who steps into the actual leadership role. You may be the one with the greatest concern, or maybe you're simply the first one who has read this book. Perhaps you are the catalyst to bring the group together, from which another person with strong up-front leadership skills will emerge.

Every movement needs an M-rivet. But then the gifts of planning, organizing, and administration must emerge intentionally in order to provide the skeletal structure and staying power. These are the gifts that take the persons and enthusiasm produced by M-rivets and apply their influence in the right places at the right time to bring about change. These are the practical persons who provide handles for action.

Again, let me say that a movement is strongest when it does not focus on one leader or become an extension of the personality of one leader. The decision-making process must be in the hands of a team of leaders. So far as possible, the leader must be a catalyst for the formation and release of the group. The key is servanthood: a leader who is committed to multiplying influence by raising up others into leadership.

THE BUILDING PROCESS

Keeping in mind certain principles that pertain to the psychology of small groups is helpful in building and strengthening any movement through the long haul. Basically, there are three virtually unavoidable stages through which every group will go:

1. *Form*—This is the organizing stage, when we build relationships, clarify goals, and establish trust and commitment. You could call it "the honeymoon period."

2. *Storm*—Here we face the difficult task of testing one another's roles, challenging the leadership, establishing ownership. It's like a young married couple's deciding how to adjust to one another's idiosyncrasies—how to squeeze the toothpaste tube and who takes out the garbage.

3. *Reform*—This is the working out of a covenant that expresses the priorities of the group. Each member discovers his niche, and working relationships are established. Here, you make the marriage that is secure.

These stages of group growth are consistent whether it's a local group made up of three or four neighbors or a movement of disgruntled farmers from all over North America. Being aware that the storm period is essential and that it is a time of positive growth will enable leaders and members to persevere through inevitable difficulties without feeling discouragement.[1]

A Lone Ranger clamps down and takes control when the storm period occurs. But a servant leader recognizes the value of the storm for discovering the various gifts in the group. He or she will be looking for other mobilizers, a long-range planner, a gifted worship leader, an organizer. He or she will want to find a person who can put the concrete plans under the vision, and someone else who has time to study resources in depth and train the group. Everyone has some gift or gifts that are needed. No one has all the gifts that are necessary.

DECISIONS BY CONSENSUS

Meeting and growing together deepen our commitment to each other and to our task, working for unity in purpose, style of leadership, and spirit. We have told one another, "We will not use one another. We will guard one another's integrity and stewardship of leadership. We will not use one another's name until we all agree on what the problem is, what the strategy is to be, and how we're going to get there. When we all buy in, we will surface as a team committed to a common good."

We have said to the leaders in our city—the civic leaders, the business leaders, and the denominational leaders—we will never use your names with anybody else unless we are given permission. And we will not emerge publicly as a group with any specific statement until we are together in our goals and strategy. Following this principle carefully strengthens the team by building trust and mutual confidence.

And by the way, one of the greatest assets of the team is that we don't face the presence of pornography alone. In our fellowship in Cincinnati, we covenant to be accountable to one another; there are no private viewings, for example, of "skin flicks." This is high-potency poison; it can kill. It has seduced and destroyed many lives. I won't look at even the printed materials for any reason without one of the team with me. I know how weak I am, and how easily I can be drawn into temptation.

We respect one another's vulnerability, and that's why a movement with accountability is absolutely essential. Together we have the ability to study the magazines, tapes, and films in a limited but adequate way, so that when we rise up to speak against a subject, we know what we're talking about.

GIVE A GOOD REPORT

In Cincinnati, we consistently practice the "Good Report Principle." That is, we have agreed to speak nothing unkind or negative about another person on the team. Our goal is that when necessary, we confront another privately with whatever is bothering us, speaking the truth in love with sensitivity and gentleness. There is no place for gossip within the team.

As we build the team against pornography there is only one object of attack: the evil we are standing against. This is not just a hundred-yard dash—we're together for a marathon. And we cannot afford to wound or undermine one another. But our primary reason for living out this principle is far more important. To wound Christians by our words is to wound Jesus and to divide His body here on earth. That is a luxury which we can't tolerate.

The Good Report Principle is a decision to prevent anything's breaking the momentum of the team, whether it be doctrinal differences, personality quirks, or a variation in style and leadership gifts.[2] When you go to war, you do not dabble with civilian life. You put pettiness and less important differences aside. Remember, we are joining together to win this battle, no matter how long that might take.

SPECTATOR—PARTICIPANT—STARTER

I was a bench-warmer in varsity basketball until my senior year in high school. At the University of Washington, I made the team but still warmed the bench. I supported the starters as an eager reserve, and I received my satisfaction from being part of the number-three team in the nation. But I warmed the bench most of the time.

For years I had a similar mentality in the ministry. I looked at the most gifted and charismatic pastors I knew and assumed I was still called to be on the second team, primarily to support and encourage those up front. There is nothing wrong with being a Barnabas, of having the gift of encouragement. What is wrong is to allow yourself to fall into a spectator mentality, relegating yourself to being second-class.

God doesn't have second- or third-string players. All of us are starters. We have different roles or functions, to be sure, and different degrees of effectiveness. But each person is placed there by God and is valuable for the success of the team. All of us are in the game. We pastors are the playing coaches. Jesus and His saints cheer us on from heaven (see Heb. 12:1, 2). And the ball is in our court.

THREE LEVELS OF INVOLVEMENT

I recognize that few people have the time or abilities to be full-time leaders in the battle against pornography, but all can be involved in some way. Steering the nation back on the road to morality will require involvement of many people at different levels. It helps to think of these various levels of involvement as three overlapping tracks:

Track No. 1—Priority Commitment. These people are the mobilizers building the team—sharing in leadership decisions, organizing specific actions, training team members, raising financial support, speaking to public and religious groups.

Track No. 2—Sense of Call. Here are the people with definite, short-term or rhythmic involvement, tackling specific projects, making frequent phone calls and writing letters regularly to businesses and officials, supporting local actions.

Track No. 3—Concern. These are individuals with heightened awareness, but with minimal activity—praying, learning the facts, signing petitions, giving financial support, encouraging the team, occasionally calling or mailing personal letters to officials when a concerted effort is necessary.

Who should be on Track No. 3?

- Those who are too busy to be more deeply involved. There are numerous other areas of ministry that deserve the primary calling of many people.

- Those who have been deeply wounded by pornography and sexual crimes, and who would suffer from more active involvement. When the wounds have healed through counseling and care in the Christian community, then there will be time to become more active, to speak out as a victim, witnessing to the dangers of pornography and showing the possibility of healing and victory.
- Those who have been victims in the sense that they have been addicted to pornography and suffer the temptations of lust. These individuals can't risk deeper involvement. Their part will be on Track 3, occasionally testifying to warn others of the dangers.
- Those who have physical limitations that prevent more active involvement.

THE PEOPLE BEHIND THE SCENES

When a local movement is in its first stages, all of the work must be done quietly away from the public eye to establish the firm foundation that public action will be built upon later. Here is a very brief outline of the people needed for behind the scenes support.

1. *People who pray*—Pray for God's plan and the power of the Holy Spirit; for protection, for perseverance, for power to persuade and prevail. Praying people can mobilize others to pray.

2. *Researchers*—Read and study the materials, articles, books, and reports, and digest and share the results with team members. Study and research take

hours of time and an aptitude for discerning facts that may be buried in rhetoric and technical jargon. We need people with the ability to sift through information and then interpret it to the team.

3. *Writers*—Choice of words can make a great difference in how a letter or article is received: "Sir, the magazines in your store are (objectionable, disgusting, dirty, indecent, inappropriate, degrading)." Each word may be accurate, but each conveys a different style. A writer on the team can prepare *model letters* (not form letters) other members can use as guidelines. Writers can draft letters to the editor and articles for periodicals and newsletters, and assist those who will be speaking to the media and public.

4. *Organizers*—The gift of administration, the ability to see what needs to be done and how to do it most effectively, is sometimes the most valuable gift a team can find.

5. *Workerbees*—These employ the gift of helps—hands to fold letters, stuff envelopes, copy phone lists, type proposals, and distribute fliers. These are the people who make phone calls or walk picket lines or join a march on City Hall. There is so much legwork, handwork, and plain nitty-gritty work necessary to make the team effort successful that the willing hands of workerbees are the key to getting things done.

6. *Financial supporters*—Significant monetary backing is needed for office space and supplies, postage, travel expenses, and a score of other things not anticipated until the bills come in. Giving people the privilege of sharing in this effort will bless those who see the problem and don't know how to change the situation. It will enable some persons to make a

meaningful difference who couldn't help any other way. So ask. As Mother Teresa of Calcutta says, "Begging is a beautiful thing when done in the name of Jesus Christ."[3]

THE PEOPLE UPFRONT

1. *Icebreakers*—These are individuals with the ability to take a strong stand for justice against powerful people. The icebreaker has guts, is willing to be different, to take a risk. This is the person willing to walk up to the manager of the neighborhood drug store, to visit the area and regional managers, and even telephone the national president, if necessary. The icebreakers will move the team from concern into action.

2. *Speakers*—Some individuals have the ability to stand in front of ten or a hundred or a thousand people and speak clearly and persuasively. The team needs several strong speakers from various denominations and political backgrounds, who can speak to the mind and stir the heart without being abrasive or antagonistic. Although sometimes the movement's spokesperson will have the title of *chairman* or *president*, it must always be clear that he or she is representing the whole team, not one person's view.

3. *Teachers*—Like the researchers, but on a broader scale, these team members offer classes to inform and equip members of the congregation or community. Teachers can equip others to be leaders by sharing their books and research materials and by "team-teaching" classes. We now have printed materials and excellent audio and videotapes of our first two Na-

tional Consultations on Pornography that can be used effectively for classes when the teacher is a "learner among learners."

4. *Multipliers*—Even those who are not comfortable teaching or speaking in front of groups can speak to their families, neighbors, and friends, sharing their concern and inviting them to join in attending classes, writing letters, and visiting merchants. The more the message is shared, the more the team is multiplied; this is the M-rivet concept.

HANDY EXCUSES

There are plenty of reasons not to get involved. Not everyone will say yes. To help you anticipate the excuses you may hear, here are several typical rationalizations.

"I'm too busy."—I used that excuse for a long time. With a congregation of twenty-one hundred members and a staff of nine full-time, ministerial level associates, I already put in a work week of seventy to eighty hours. My five children, four grandchildren, and my wife Patty all deserve more attention than I can possibly give them. But precisely because I love my congregation and family, I had to make time to do something against pornography. How much time do you have? Twenty-four hours per day, the same as every other person. The only difference is how we choose to use that time.

"I don't have the abilities."—None of us has enough ability. That's why our Lord sent the Holy Spirit to equip and empower and train us to do His work. You have the ability in God's power to do whatever it is

that God wants to accomplish through you. You only have to be willing and available, and He will make you adequate to the task.

"I don't know what to do."—Here's good news: most of the groundwork has been laid and the organizations established. Just call or write to one of the groups listed in the appendix, and they'll get you started with the materials needed to establish a knowledge base and a project that you can handle.

"I can't get out of the house."—Much of the work can be done in the house. You can make phone calls, write letters, offer to fold and label newsletters for a local group, read books and articles, and compose articles and proposals, pray for the national effort, pray for the local effort, pray for the victims and the victimizers and the children and the doctors and the prosecutors and the jurists. Pray, and then pray some more! You'll be amazed by the doors that the Lord will open to you.

"I don't have the right to impose my morality on others."—You're right. Nor do pornographers have the right to impose their *immorality* on others. This is the whole point of the movement. We are not trying to impose our morality on others; we are trying to see that existing laws are enforced. Our form of democracy puts the responsibility clearly on the shoulders of citizens to work for the common good and a high quality of life in our communities and nation. Jesus called this being salt and light to the world.

"They are too many; we are too few."—The pornographers would like to have us believe that, but it's a lie.

Yes, there is much obscenity on the market, and, yes, there's big money behind it. But claiming that most Americans want pornography or that obscenity is acceptable to society is a lie. We've seen that when communities discover the danger in pornography and the truth about the law and obscenity, great numbers of enraged citizens rise up and succeed in calling a halt to its distribution. It's happened already in Cincinnati, Orlando, Fort Wayne, Atlanta, Pittsburgh, and numerous other cities. And it can happen in your community, if you are willing to make it happen.

"If I say to the wicked, 'You shall surely die,' and you give him no warning, nor speak to warn the wicked from his wicked way, in order to save his life, that wicked man shall die in his iniquity, but his blood I will require at your hand" (Ezek. 3:18).

A WOMAN WHO MADE A DIFFERENCE

One woman, Tanya Chalupa, began a campaign in 1978 to enact legislation in California that would require safety restraints in automobiles for children under four years old and less than forty pounds. Her family had been in a terrifying accident and she was convinced that her child had survived only by being restrained in a car seat.

She discovered that 90 percent of childhood highway deaths and 60 percent of injuries could be prevented with the use of car seats. Because she cared not only for her own child but for all the children in her community, Tanya researched other states' laws, organized phone networks, lobbied state senators, and worked with a children's rights organization.

It took four years, but in January 1983, the Child Restraint Law went into effect in California. And in the past year, an estimated three hundred children have been saved from injury and death. Because of that one person, other states have already passed similar laws.[4]

Evil abounds in our society, not because there are no concerned Christians but because so many Christians do nothing. Or perhaps they do a little and then get tired and frustrated and give up. We need tenacity! It's ultimately of less importance how big a group we have than how committed we are to the vision and to one another. So we build the team, we establish commitment, and then we move.

ENDNOTES

1. Additional references on group building: Elizabeth O'Connor, *Journey Inward, Journey Outward* (New York: Harper and Row, 1968).

Mary Cosby, *Building a Multiple-Dimensional Group*—a Group on Mission (tape), Word Publishing.

Charles Olsen, *The Church in Small Groups* (tape and manual), Forum House/Word.

2. Two taped messages that are helpful in this area are *The Good Report* by Rev. Ron Rand, and *Fellowship* by Dr. Richard Halverson. Both are available through College Hill Presbyterian Church, Tape Ministry, 5742 Hamilton Avenue, Cincinnati, Ohio, 45224.

3. Malcolm Muggeridge, *Something Beautiful for God, Mother Teresa of Calcutta* (Garden City, N.Y.: Doubleday, 1977), 48-49.

4. Melinda Welsh, "Spare the Cuddle and Save the Child," *Family Circle*, Oct. 23, 1984, 16.

Chapter 9

An Individual Game Plan

Right here we must see the difference between choosing to serve and choosing to be a servant. When we choose to serve we are still in charge. We decide who we will serve and when we will serve. And if we are in charge we will worry a great deal about anyone's stepping on us, i.e., taking charge over us.

But when we choose to be a servant we give up the right to be in charge. There is a great freedom in this.... When we choose to be a servant we surrender the right to decide who and when we will serve. We become available and vulnerable.

Richard Foster, *Celebration of Discipline*, 115

There are times when, viewing the pervading immorality in our culture, nearly everyone feels like an insignificant cog in a vast machine of gear wheels. In this particular nation at this particular time, the power of one person to make significant change in national policies is widely misunderstood.

Having said that, I admit that facing the onslaught of pornography is like facing a tidal wave—the primary concern is survival rather than stopping the terrible momentum. It seems that nothing can stand in the way of this avalanche of filth; I know that feeling and have heard it expressed by most of the people whom I have contacted.

But we often use our sense of powerlessness as an excuse for avoiding personal responsibility, presuming that we are helpless to change things. Let me give you an illustration of what one letter, written by Bill Kelly, accomplished.

Kelly, you will recall, is the retired F.B.I. agent whose specialty was the investigation of the pornography industry run by organized crime.

In the spring of 1984, he was at the Harley Hotel on Forty-second Avenue in New York City for the National Catholic Conference on the Illegal Sex Industry. At the convenience shop in the hotel lobby, Bill found four or five of the leading soft-porn magazines on display: *Playboy, Penthouse,* and others.

Bill decided to take specific action, not as an F.B.I. agent, but simply as a concerned private citizen. He went back to his room, took the comment card provided in the desk, and wrote a polite, specific note expressing his objection to their selling pornography in the lobby, stating that such merchandise was completely out of place in such a high-class hotel.

Within two weeks, Bill received a reply from Leona M. Helmsley, president of the Harley Hotels, thanking him for his concern and expressing her total agreement and commitment to remove all such magazines not only from that hotel, but also from all of the hotels in their nationwide chain.

Then, in November, Bill was asked to speak at the First Presbyterian Church of Orlando, and stayed at the Harley there. Checking the newspaper stand in that lobby, he again found pornography. This time, instead of the "comments card," he sat down and wrote a personal letter. The response, received even more quickly than the first, written on Mrs. Helmsley's personal stationery, was sincere in thanking him for his concern. She expressed shock about the magazines being for sale and assured him that the condition had been unintentional on the part of the hotel management. The newsstands and candy counters in the chain of hotels were operated by an independent concessionaire, and generally the hotel management did not oversee their merchandise. Mrs. Helmsley reaffirmed her position to have all objectionable materials removed from the Harley Hotels. We thank you, Mrs. Helmsley, and we are counting on you.

You don't have to be an F.B.I. special investigator to write a letter, just a concerned citizen. One letter can make the difference.

THE POWER OF THE WRITTEN WORD

We are told that politicians assume that each letter represents the thoughts and opinions of one hundred of their constituents. This gives some idea of the importance of a letter. Personal letters, thoughtfully, carefully, sensitively written, have great power.

Underline the word *personal*. Form letters don't have the same effect. They are better than nothing at all, but they express a "me, too" mentality and draw attention to an organized effort. A personal letter, one that reflects careful thought, growing out of intense personal concern, is taken seriously and is usually answered personally. It becomes part of that office's continuing file and heightens the official's awareness, which is just what you're trying to do.

Also underline the word *sensitively*. We need to write in such a way that those who receive our letters are aware that we have given the matter serious thought and that we believe they will receive our letter with equal seriousness.

May I remind you that not only should you write personal letters, but you can multiply your influence considerably by recruiting others who will also write personal letters. They might want to see yours as an illustration, but be sure that they are instructed to write theirs in such a way that they are unique and personal.

WHEN YOU CARE ENOUGH...
SEND THE VERY BEST

1. Prepare yourself thoroughly through prayer and careful study to write your letter.

2. Begin with clarity of purpose in your mind and communicate that purpose early in the letter. Don't waste your reader's time.

3. Write to the person at the top or as close to the top as you can get. Show respect in your words and attitude by taking your reader seriously, recognizing his or her role and authority, and by showing deference when appropriate. Dr. Richard Halverson, chaplain of the Senate, told Presbyterians at the Congress on Renewal that the spirit of a letter is as important as the content. "Christians should reflect the love and caring of Jesus Christ in how they say something as well as what they say."

4. Write with gentleness and sensitivity, with strength and tenacity. Assume the person receiving your letter is in agreement with your purpose and give him or her the benefit of the doubt. The person you are writing to may not know the dangers of pornography or be aware of his own company's participation. Present yourself as an ally.

5. Important—a one-page, three- or four-paragraph letter is always best.

6. Read every letter aloud before it's sent. Better still, ask someone else to read it to you. Does it really say what you intend it to say? Be open to any suggestions trusted friends might make. "In an abundance of counselors there is safety" (Prov. 11:14).

7. Never, ever, deal with more than one issue per letter, or its impact will be lost. Your reader is too busy already, so protect his time.

THE ELEVENTH HOUR FOR 7-ELEVEN

Assuming that it will be helpful for you to see a sample letter, on the following pages you will find the text of a letter I wrote to Mr. John Thompson of Dallas, Texas. Mr. Thompson is president of Southland, parent company of 7-Eleven stores, at this writing the largest seller of pornographic magazines in the United States.

The letter was signed by every member of the session of College Hill Presbyterian Church, and copies were sent to every member of the Southland board of directors. Study carefully; the letter is respectful, and focused on one issue. My communication with Mr. Thompson is a much stronger letter than I would usually write on a first occasion. This is because Mr. Thompson had received numerous letters and personal visits from other persons. My letter was one of a number of contacts.

Dear Mr. Thompson,
I am pastor of a two thousand-member Presbyterian congregation in Cincinnati, Ohio, and have purchased gas and many other items quite regularly in your 7-Eleven Convenient Stores for years. However, I

want you and your board of directors to know that I am withdrawing all my business from your stores because of your obvious commitment to promote drugs and promiscuous sex among young people and married people in our communities.

In recent months I have, for the first time, read *Playboy, Penthouse, Forum,* and other magazines that you sell in your stores. I am appalled at the message of those magazines and the way they degrade women and mock marital fidelity. Mr. Thompson, I have great difficulty believing that you believe in promoting those things and the destruction of family life in America. I have great difficulty believing you and your board of directors are not becoming increasingly aware of the terrible impact of pornography as evidenced in the growing sexual revolution, and the fruit of that in the abuse of women through rape, and of children through sexual abuse and other forms of violence.

Sir, have you seen the magazines that your stores are selling in neighborhoods and communities all across this land? Have you read the newspapers to see the growing rate of rape and abuse in homes? Have you read the statistics to know how many of those homes have contained pornographic magazines when the police arrested the people? Is it possible that you care more about the money you are making than about the people's lives you are helping to destroy? Does it give you pleasure that you are the largest seller of pornography in America?

I want you to know that all of my five children join me in sending this letter. Two are married and have children and one will be married next month. I want you to know that the officers and leaders of my congregation join me in this appeal to you. And after having spent hours and hours and hours counseling young people with herpes, with unexpected pregnancies out of wedlock, and/or persons who are violated by their own fathers because their fathers were reading pornographic magazines, I am ready to tell every person I can, everywhere, please to join with us to do all that they can to help preserve family life in America and to help young people establish responsible sexual morals which your company is helping to tear down.

I have never before written the president of a company to plead with him to take a costly moral stand—costly in terms of dollars and cents, but priceless in terms of the value and worth of persons.

Mr. Thompson, you have the opportunity to help redeem the past by giving moral leadership within the business community of this nation. I ask you, in the name of decency, to do so. I urge you, in the name of compassion, please do so. The moral rage and reaction to pornography is growing in America among Presbyterians, Episcopalians, Roman Catholics, Lutherans, Baptists, Nazarenes, Assemblies of God and the Jewish Community. We will take our message to America with you or without you. I hope, very much, that it will be with your help and support.

I look forward to hearing from you and from your board members to whom I am sending a copy of this letter.

Yours,
Jerry R. Kirk, Pastor
cc: Members of the Board of Directors,
Southland Corporation

You can help this particular effort, by the way, in visiting a 7-Eleven store in your community. If it is not selling any objectionable material, go to the manager and thank him or her. Ask if the national management has changed its policy.

The Mind Polluters

But if the magazines are still there, let the manager know that you believe this is inappropriate merchandise for your neighborhood, and indicate your intention to refuse to patronize that store as long as it contributes to the destruction of family life by continuing to sell magazines that promote promiscuity and infidelity. Then immediately send off a personal letter to Mr. Thompson, clearly stating your concern.

One letter per week is a workable, effective habit, and through it you can influence a vast number of leaders. Merchants, advertisers, political leaders, and law enforcement officials are all accessible through the mail. They properly place considerable importance on personal correspondence. As you become more proficient and experienced, you'll be developing communication channels with many influential people over a short period of time.

Again, do not underestimate your potential influence. I had always assumed I could never write a letter to the editor or get my views into print. But when I became so deeply moved over the scourge of obscenity that I had to write, my letter was printed on the editorial page, as were many others. Basically, a letter to the editor is much the same as the letters we've already discussed. Think over carefully what you want to say and keep in mind the people you expect to read the letter. What are the necessary facts to support your argument? What should the reader do because of it? Ask a friend or team member to help evaluate the text before you offer it to the press.

A surprisingly easy step is to telephone the editorial staff of the local paper and simply ask what points they look for in a good letter and what you can do to meet their expectations. Someone in your congregation, P.T.A., or social group may work at the paper or know someone who does. Ask for their help. Let them know why you are so deeply concerned, so that they will be motivated to work with you, expanding the team. This can even inspire them to write a letter of their own.

Look around for other avenues for expression. Church newsletters, corporation in-house publications, P.T.A. papers, and local professional journals are usually staffed by volunteers who are eager for articles on subjects of deep concern to their members, especially if voiced by the members themselves. A church newsletter reaches every family of the congregation, out-of-town members, young people at college, mission workers overseas. A P.T.A. newspaper is carried home from school by every child. An article in your company's quarterly may be read by thousands of employees. Call up the editors and explain what you want to write and why. They'll be pleased to help you.

SHOW THEM YOU CARE—CALL

The principles that distinguish a good letter also apply to a good phone call. Be prepared factually and spiritually, be kind and brief, and come right to the point of the call. Keep Jesus' advice in the Golden Rule before you, and respect the authority of the one to whom you speak.

Cultivate the gift of calling by phoning different persons of influence in the community, both political and business leaders, to engender support for halting pornography. Because we learn by doing, calling gets easier and easier. In fact, it becomes enjoyable and rewarding as you gain experience in dealing with people over the phone. Encourage and train others to do the same, and you will see your impact multiplied.

Kari discovered first-hand the power of a personal phone call. She had attended the first National Consultation on Pornography and Obscenity in Cincinnati in 1983, and was shocked when she saw the materials being marketed by pornographers. She was moved to tears and then to action.

When she returned to Louisville, Kentucky, where she lives with her husband and two children, she recruited a neighbor and together they visited six drugstores and convenience shops in their community. They found three stores which did not carry sexual literature, and to each of these managers Kari wrote a personal letter of commendation and appreciation.

But they found one drugstore that was selling "men's magazines." Kari spoke with the manager, who was sympathetic with her concern, and obtained the name and phone number of the drugstore owner. For three days Kari tried unsuccessfully to reach him. But she refused to give up, even though she had that uneasy feeling every time she picked up the phone.

When Kari finally reached him, this is how the conversation went: "Sir, are you Mr. _____ ?"

"Yes."

"Are you the owner of _____ drugstore at the corner of Race and Roosevelt?"

"Yes, I am."

"Sir, I'm a customer of your drugstore, and I've spent sixteen dollars on prescriptions in the past three weeks. And I wondered if I could ask you some questions?"

"Certainly, how can I help you?"

"Sir, do you believe that teen-agers in our community should be encouraged to be promiscuous in their sexual activity and in their use of drugs?"

"No, of course not!"

"Do you respect those who are influencing the breakdown of marriages in our community?"

"No! I'm a family man, and I don't want to see the breakdown of family life."

"Then, sir, why do you sell in your store pornographic magazines that clearly promote promiscuous sex and drug use among teen-agers and married people?"

His response was that no one had ever asked him that question before, and so Kari went on.

"Sir, as I said earlier, I have patronized your drugstore in the past three weeks, but I'm not going to spend another penny there as long as you sell those magazines that are undermining the moral strength of our community. And I feel so strongly about this, I am going to tell all my friends to join with me in buying from other drugstores as long as you sell such materials.

"I've thought a great deal about this and felt constrained to call you because I was sent as a customer to your store by my Christian doctor, who told me that he had confidence in you and your integrity. I am going to call my doctor, tell him what you are selling in your store, and request that he send no more persons in as customers. This may seem harsh, but the well-being of my family and of other families is worth that much to me."

There was only a brief silence. Then the man on the other end of the line asked if Kari would give him her name and phone number, which she did.

About an hour later on that same day, Kari answered a phone call and was surprised to find it was the drugstore manager. "Our owner has asked me to tell you that we are removing all the pornographic magazines from our drugstore. He also wanted me to thank you and to say that he's removing those same magazines from the other two drugstores he owns as well."

Kari, a determined young mother, made one phone call that made the difference.

For many of us, fear keeps us from making that first phone call. For some of us, fear would have kept us from the second or the third call which ultimately produced the results. But remember, "God did not give us a spirit of timidity but a spirit of power and love and self-control" (2 Tim. 1:7).

From Kari's experience, we can see she was prepared. She knew what she wanted to say and how she was going to say it. She went to the top and gave the owner the opportunity to take the position of a family man who was concerned about his own children. And she established a basis for him to respect her as a customer. She made it clear that he was not the object of complaint, but the merchandise. I know these details well, for dear Kari is my own daughter.

One well-prepared phone call can have big results. How many magazines will not be sold or read because of that call?

Certain people are more accessible by phone than by mail, and the immediate quality of a personal telephone conversation often has a stronger effect. The receiver of your call discerns your sincerity, integrity, and friendship by the tone of your voice. And, of course, following up a letter with a phone call underscores the urgency of your point.

The reverse is also true, incidentally. Following up a phone call with a brief note underscores the depth of your concern and brings back to mind the impact of your call.

FACE TO FACE

When our Cincinnati team was just beginning to consider doing something beyond praying and studying, Ethel Seifert, a housewife and a retired executive secretary, spoke up. "Well, let's go talk to some city council members. Who can go with me next Tuesday?"

We all just stared in disbelief and someone said aloud, "Who, us?"

"Of course, us!"

Over ten years ago, Ethel had been active in the civil-rights movement in Cincinnati and had learned how effective visits with politicians could be. So she taught us how to approach the council members and to catch the attention of the people in power.

After much prayer, it became apparent that our timidity was a similar fear that prevents many Christians from openly sharing their faith with others. Far from acting like fanatics, we could learn to speak out with respect, gentleness, and love. We read the Scriptures and prayed for each other.

I admit that I struggled with that first visit. But being the pastor, I assumed that I needed to help set an example! Kathy Woods, our local chairperson, confessed the same feelings.

"I'm chicken," she said. "I want people to like me, and if I show my face down at city hall, my friends will think I'm some kind of nut!"

We talked and supported one another. We reassured

ourselves that the real "nut" was anyone who wouldn't speak out against immorality and the prime promoters of the sexual revolution.

To our great surprise—and relief—the city council leaders met us graciously, listened carefully to our concerns, and began to give the issue serious attention. Steps were taken in Cincinnati through the county prosecutor and city council toward stopping the *Playboy* Channel and passing a "display law."

Later, we were encouraged to continue our visits and to make additional appointments with heads of corporations and media people. It isn't easy to this day, but as we keep going, we gain confidence in the process and in our own abilities. Also, our influence is growing.

Let me repeat: don't ever let your initial hesitancy keep you from that first visit. Through this book I can help equip you with ideas to maximize your success. But remember, you don't learn to visit by reading. You learn by going. Choose a person who is most likely to be open and supportive for the first visit, because it's that first visit that will be the most difficult. From then on it gets easier.

Dr. Edgar Johnson, executive director of the Church of the Nazarene, had bought gas at the same service station for some seventeen years. One day he discovered that they had added pornographic magazines to their shelves. He asked to speak to the manager.

"I have been purchasing gas at your station for some seventeen years," Dr. Johnson told the manager. "I've appreciated the service that I have received. However, I realized just today that you have begun selling sexually explicit and pornographic magazines.

I believe so deeply that this material is promoting a lifestyle destructive to individuals and to family life that as long as you sell that material, I will no longer be buying gasoline from this station."

Two or three weeks later, Dr. Johnson stopped by that service station again. He found that the magazines were still there. He wrote a brief note to the manager:

> Dear Mr. _____ , I noticed today that you are still selling the magazines, and I wanted to remind you that as long as this merchandise is being sold in this store, I will have to take my business elsewhere out of personal conviction. Thank you for your attention to this matter.

On four or five different occasions during a three-month period, he came back, wrote a brief note from a slightly different perspective, respectfully indicating regret that they were selling such magazines.

On the sixth visit, he discovered that the station had been remodeled and that all of the pornographic magazines were gone. He asked the salesperson and found they had indeed been removed. Dr. Johnson said, "Well, then, please fill up my van out there!" It amounted to about thirty dollars worth of gas at one shot! Then he wrote a final note to the manager, thanking him for his cooperation and for his moral stand.

This is the kind of thing one person can do. If you think through the way you're going to do it, and if you do it in a way that genuinely respects the integrity and the responsibility of the other person, results will begin to come.

TWO BY TWO

The same principles that apply to letters and phone calls apply to personal visits—clarity of purpose, thorough preparation, respect for authority, sensitivity, brevity, and single-mindedness. For visiting, add courage to the list!

The advantage of working with a team is really apparent when you begin visiting authorities in person. Jesus sent the apostles out two by two, and that's an example well worth following. Whenever possible, make the visit with a team member who has experience, and let that partner take the lead, even if you were the one who initiated the visit. But go with no more than one or occasionally two partners, or the individual you visit may feel defensive and intimidated.

It is best to go by appointment, showing respect for the busy schedule of the person you visit. Be sensitive to the fact that your concern about pornography is just one element in the broad spectrum of issues that he or she has to consider. Retailers are the one possible exception to the appointment principle. It's sometimes easier for a store manager to speak with you briefly on the spot than it is to set up a later appointment. Be sure to ask which arrangement the manager prefers.

After each visit, evaluate your experience with the team and plan the next visit to another official or executive in the light of that evaluation. Remember, we're in this for the long haul. View each visit both as a learning experience and as an opportunity for building a team of effective visitors. As two or three partners become proficient, they can split into separate teams and couple with two other less experienced partners, so that the teams grow slowly and solidly.

At times we have done more listening than speaking, and this is almost always the best approach. Sometimes we find that by briefly expressing our concern and allowing a response, that person will talk around the subject and end up agreeing with our point of view. Chances are that the individual hadn't thought the issue through thoroughly before. Even when the person visited can't respond positively to our purpose, we make certain that he or she can respond positively to us.

THREE RESPONSES

You will encounter three types of people as you visit:

(1) those who are already concerned about the problem and are encouraged and strengthened by our support;

(2) those who don't have strong convictions one way or another on the issue and are open to being informed through us;

(3) those who are opposed to our point of view.

This last group of individuals needs to be convinced that its electorate or clientele is strongly united against pornography. If they are politically and/or economically sensitive, they may be moved to change their position. Those who initially stand firmly against our persuasion are often moved to alter their stance for the sake of their own advantage.

In the earlier chapter on the legal aspects of opposing pornography, you will remember that the Supreme Court's definition of the term *obscenity* relates to "community standards." What is the process that helps to establish those standards in each community? *Community people's visiting their representatives and clearly expressing their concerns.* Period.

Our political system is a democracy, which gives the power for directing the government to the people. Elected officials appear distant and unapproachable partly because people cower in the face of their authority. So be politely bold! Elected officials are eager to hear the concerns of their constituents. Never hesitate to make yourself heard and to learn to use the power that is rightly yours. As one bumper sticker says, "I am against pornography, and I vote!"

This was our strategy in the case concerning the "display law" established here in Cincinnati. The display law was an attempt to have all "adult" magazines placed out of the reach of children and young people who might pick them up and browse through them. The law would also require opaque shields over the magazines so that the cover pictures would not be exposed to youngsters. First, we researched similar laws in other states. Then we began to meet with the various city council members to learn their positions on the issue. We discovered that four of the nine people on city council were in favor of such a law. This led us to a series of hearings and letters to the editor so that the debate was taking place citywide as well.

The outcome of this activity was that we obtained the help of some of the city council members in rewriting the display law. In order to gain the support of one council member to swing the vote to our side, that part of the law that required all such magazines to be covered was passed by one vote and the part that limited access to such materials by minors was not passed. Never underestimate the impact you can have with politicians through personal visits.

In Cincinnati, our letters, phone calls, and visits all have had good results. It has taken patience and persistence, but we have realized a good measure of success, and we are continuing our efforts. But what if in spite of hundreds of letters, dozens of phone calls, and repeated visits to authorities, pornography stays on the shelves, "adult" bookstores stay in business, and X-rated theaters thrive? What can your community do should all these efforts fail?

Chapter 10

Strategies for Teams

William Wilberforce, eighteenth century slave trade aboli-
tionist, wrote in his diary: "God Almighty has set before
me two great objects, the suppression of the slave trade
and the reformation of manners." The latter did not refer to
table etiquette, of course, but to the moral standards of pro-
fessing Christians.
Wilberforce believed holy living, what he called the "refor-
mation of manners," would inevitably foster righteousness
in the land and end the injustice of slavery; conversely, the
end of slavery would uplift the moral character of the na-
tion.
That is precisely what happened. Slavery was abolished as
a great spiritual awakening swept England clean of its in-
dulgent apostasy.

Charles Colson, Loving God, 141

SLOPPY AGAPE OR LIBERATING LOVE?

Jesus loved by both His words and actions. He wasn't reticent about confronting unbelief, whether it was selfishness in the apostles or hypocrisy in the Pharisees. His love was "tough love."

"Sloppy agape," on the other hand, refuses to address personal moral values revealed by God or to call each other to accountability. Instead, this sentimental love allows each individual to do his own thing in the name of freedom. It's the attitude that says, "That's OK, God doesn't expect you to be perfect." The Old Testament called it doing what is right in your own eyes. It is a love that does not liberate.

Jesus never displayed that kind of love because it isn't love at all. Sloppy agape leaves people in the bondage of guilt and shame. It's the antithesis of godly love.

The difficult question is, do we love people enough to confront sin? Do we take people's lives and their sin seriously enough to call them to repentance, forgiveness, and healing? Do we respect others enough to let them know their actions are harming people and placing themselves in mortal danger?

Jesus put His love into action. His love to sinners was gentle and kind. He loved them by taking time to listen. He made people feel worthwhile. In His presence, people had significance and usefulness. He taught and He lived as though every person was important, having dignity and worth, including women, children, the sick and the poor. But His love was demanding. After teaching and modeling righteousness, Jesus took dramatic, specific action.

THE HARD SAYING OF JESUS

In the temple he found those who were selling oxen and sheep and pigeons, and the money-changers at their business. And making a whip of cords, he drove them all, with the sheep and oxen, out of the temple; and he poured out the coins of the money-changers and overturned their tables. And he told those who sold the pigeons, "Take these things away; you shall not make my Father's house a house of trade" (John 2:14-16).

Jesus took sin, the honor of God, and the truth of God seriously. The people He acted against were those who were making economic profit from sin—those who had desecrated something sacred for financial gain.

Sex was created by God for a sacred place within marriage. But pornographers have desecrated sex by perverting it for financial gain. They make economic profit from the sin of those who want to look at indecency. Owners and managers of stores and corporations that sell obscenity are debasing the dignity of women and children. If we love as Jesus Christ commanded us to love, we will take dramatic, specific action.

SPEAKING THE SAME LANGUAGE

What motivates businessmen to market pornographic materials? The answer is very basic: profit. The marketplace knows only one language, and that's the language of economics: the bottom line. Retailers carry smut because it makes them money; it is, as they say, "good for business." The community needs to make smut bad for business. To do that involves the power of the dollar.[1]

More than a century ago, an English land agent named Charles Cunningham Boycott refused to accept rent at rates set by his Irish tenants. As a result, his tenants would have nothing to do with him. It took nine hundred soldiers to protect the Orangemen that came to help him harvest his crops.

It's no wonder, then, that *boycott* continues to

mean "concerted social ostracism" by a community against one of its own members as a mark of disapproval. The practice here in America actually predates the term established in Ireland. American farmers refused to use certain railroads back in the nineteenth century unless the rates were lowered. Later in the 1800s, boycotting began to be used by labor groups.

Then came product boycotting with its "fair" and "unfair" lists and secondary boycotting of organized labor against management. The typical boycott was clearly designed as economic coercion, seeking the personal financial benefit of the employee against the employer. This eventually brought about the enactment of the Taft-Hartley Act of 1947, and its section on boycotting, which made it illegal for anybody to engage in any strike or boycott that violates the principle of free enterprise.

The consumer boycott as economic persuasion against pornography seeks no personal financial benefit for the persons boycotting or necessarily the economic peril of those merchandising the material. Therefore, the negative aspects associated with boycotting as practiced by labor organizations in the past century do not apply. Much to the contrary, the boycott against pornography is a legal call for the enforcement of laws and values in the marketplace against the panderers of material that is degrading and destructive to persons and society.

When done peacefully, boycotting violates no law and deprives nobody of constitutional rights. The freedom of the seller cannot override the freedom of the buyer to purchase (or not to purchase). While the seller is free to advertise the value of his product, the consumer is free to advertise the negative impact of that product. Boycotting is high-visibility counteradvertising by the consumer. The community is free to make its choice accordingly.

WHY SHOULD THE CHRISTIAN COMMUNITY BOYCOTT?

1. The right to do so is protected by law. Conditions outlined in existing legislation against boycotting do not apply. We are exercising our American freedom to express our desire for the law to be enforced in the marketplace of free enterprise.

2. In the case of the broadcast media, producers are free to test the market for all they can gain in profit. Boycotting is one major means by which the public is able to make its marketing preferences and convictions known in the absence of regulations.

3. Moral and spiritual values of our Judeo-Christian heritage have underpinned our society from the beginning. They have been sabotaged in the name of freedom of expression. The economic boycott is an attempt to use our freedom of expression to gain back these values. In the case of films, broadcasting, and cable television, studies clearly show that much of the media is controlled by people without the religious and moral convictions common to the society they penetrate.[2] Religious and moral appeals are a language they do not understand. Therefore, we are limited to the use of the dialect of economics—which they understand very well.

4. Proper use of the boycott demonstrates, rather than threatens, the freedom we possess in America. The producers of porn are free to merchandise their

product to those who have the perverted sense to want it, if it is not obscene and contrary to federal, state, or local obscenity laws. But they have no right or freedom to seduce or to incite passion beyond the point of control in those who investigate out of curiosity. They have no freedom to spread their filth in the public domain where parents can no longer monitor what their children see and hear and do.

Those of us who are seriously concerned for the safety of our children and the moral tone of our communities are obligated to exercise our freedoms in such a manner that makes the marketplace hear and understand our value system. Unless we do, the pornographers are free and we are bound.

HOW SHOULD WE BOYCOTT PORNOGRAPHY?

First, we keep in mind that an economic boycott, or selective buying, is necessary only when all other possible methods have been used and when corporate leaders (or retail owners) have indicated a firm resolve not to act in a responsible manner for the good of the community. Letters, mass mailings, personal visits, dialogue, intercession through business organizations or community forums all must be exhausted before agressive economic steps are considered. But if all else fails, we must commit ourselves to dramatic action.

Second, we make it clear that we have no desire to hurt the corporations or their employees or the owners of individual stores or franchises. We want the cooperation of these people to help influence the corporate policy. Our goal isn't to punish retailers or gain some kind of moral one-upmanship, but to insist that the laws against obscenity are enforced and to uphold the safety and decency of the community.

Third, we establish definite, achievable goals. It may be to have certain magazines removed completely from a particular store. Or, it may be to have magazines removed from open racks and kept under the counter. In other cases, the goal may be to have explicit videotapes removed from rental outlets or to eliminate adult programming from cable television in a particular area. Whatever the target, be certain the goal is defined in specific terms so that both the distributor and the public know exactly what issue is at stake.

Fourth, in beginning a boycott, we are obligated to follow through with the boycott until our goals are achieved. Halfhearted efforts not only fail to remove pornography, but encourage the distributors that their resistance will be rewarded. If the team isn't committed to carry out the boycott for at least a year and longer if necessary, it would be better not to boycott at all.

We must mount such community outcry that dealers lose far more money by selling pornography than they lose by eliminating it from their shelves.

SPECIFIC IDEAS

King Kwik convenience stores here in Cincinnati sell pornographic magazines. United Dairy Farmers convenience stores don't sell pornography. Our team decided we would all write the president of United Dairy Farmers, thanking him for his commitment not to sell pornographic magazines and indicating that we were withdrawing all of our business from King

Kwik stores because they are promoting the destruction of family life through selling explicit sexual material. We stated our intention not to do any more business with King Kwik or 7-Eleven until they withdrew the magazines, and we would go out of our way to shop at United Dairy Farmers.

Then we sent a copy of that letter to the president of King Kwik stores and to local 7-Eleven managers, as well as to the president of United Dairy Farmers.

Whenever you go into a 7-Eleven convenience store, or a drugstore, or a book or card shop, look to see what kind of magazines are on display. If there are no pornographic magazines, tell the cashier that you appreciate their policy and express your appreciation for their high standards to the manager.

But if you do find pornographic magazines, pick up one or two and take them to the counter. Speak to the manager if he or she is there. Let the manager know that your business will go elsewhere because of that store's willingness to endanger the children and families of your community by selling pornography.

Don't be impolite. Say, "I like your store, and I appreciate having a place close by where I can get milk (or whatever their specialty is) at decent prices. But I need to tell you that these magazines are inappropriate in our neighborhood. You have a nice store, and you don't need to carry this kind of crummy thing. You probably don't realize what's in these magazines, but I don't want my kids coming in here as long as you carry this material. I'm sorry, but we'll have to shop somewhere else."

The manager will probably be very polite and appreciate your concern. But sometimes a manager will be rude or tell you that no one has ever complained before. There are those who want you to think that you're an oddball, that nobody else in the world is offended. Remember, you control what's really important to that manager...your money. Let him or her know very clearly that you will take your money elsewhere until the pornography is removed. Mention that you'll be talking to your friends about the store's policies.

Then take the time to recruit other people to visit that same store during the following weeks and months.

Another idea is this: Japanese car manufacturers, including Honda, Datsun/Nissan, and Toyota, are among the biggest advertisers in pornographic magazines in the world.

If you own a Japanese car, and if you like it, make a copy of the owner's sheet, and send it to the auto-maker with this kind of letter:

> I really like my Toyota, and I want you to know it's the best little car I've owned. It handles well, it saves me money on gas, and it seldom gives me any trouble. My wife needs a car this year, and my boy will be sixteen in two years, and I'd like to get Toyotas for both of them.
>
> But I want you to know that I'm never going to buy another Toyota as long as you continue to destroy the family life of America by advertising in pornographic magazines. By advertising in pornography, your corporation implicitly supports illicit sex and the destruction of traditional morality in America which is devastating the young people and marriages of our communities.
>
> I like Toyotas. But I also love my family. I urge you to change your marketing policies so that these two statements will no longer be in conflict.

Some of us don't own Japanese cars. Here is an example of an angry letter:

> Mister, I'd like to buy a Honda, but I can't. You have the gall to destroy the families of America and of my community and of my congregation by promoting Hondas through advertising in pornographic smut, and I'm not going to buy one until you change your advertising policy! And I'm going to tell all my friends not to buy your cars!

That letter is an example of what *not* to write. Anger begets anger. Angry people dig in their heels and defend their positions. We want to speak with reason to evoke responsible action. So a better letter to Honda would run like this:

> I need to buy a car this year. I've looked at Hondas and would prefer a Prelude or an Accord, but I can't bring myself to buy one, not because of any fault in the car. I'm convinced Honda is the best buy on the market.
>
> I can't buy a Honda because of your policy of advertising in pornographic magazines. The immorality and hedonistic philosophy of these publications undercuts the safety and sanctity of family life. Your advertising investment in pornography implicitly supports that lifestyle and all that it represents.
>
> Our families and communities are suffering the impact of illicit sex-related illnesses and crime. I cannot ignore the impact of pornography, and I cannot lend my financial approval to its supporters. I urge your company to consider the implications of your marketing practices and to take responsible steps to correct it. A quality product deserves quality advertising.

Consumer action, carried out in the right spirit with the right motive for the right issue, can alter the direction of marketing locally, nationally, and internationally. It takes effort, time, and commitment, but it works.

PICKETING...WHO, ME?

Shortly after a porn shop opened down the block from his church in Fort Wayne, Indiana, Rev. Bob Yawberg came to attorney Tom Blee for help and advice. Tom had been involved in fighting pornography in Fort Wayne for a number of years. Tom advised, "I think direct action would help better than anything else. I'd like you and your congregation to picket that joint and let's see what happens."[3]

Bob came back a couple of weeks later. "My congregation decided that we're going to pray for the conversion of that porn shop operator instead."

Tom didn't say so, but he thought privately that if the Holy Spirit changed that operator, it would put the conversion of St. Paul in the shade. Without being cynical about the power of prayer, he mused, sometimes it needs a bolt of lightning along with it.

So after many months of waiting while their prayer washed up against the hard rock of a pornographer's heart, Bob Yawberg came back to Tom again. They talked about strategy, and they called some other pastors and concerned leaders of the community, and Citizens for Decency Through Law of Fort Wayne was formed. One of their major, most effective tools was picketing.

WHY DO PEOPLE PICKET?

Only intense motivation can overcome our fears of being misunderstood, of being different, of appearing kooky, unbalanced, overzealous, misguided, and all those other nasty words that come to mind.

People picket when they believe an injustice is being perpetrated—that the law is being broken and it's time somebody did something about it.

People picket when they're being hurt by something or somebody and when they decide they don't want to be hurt anymore.

People picket when others whom they know and love and are committed to are being hurt, and they care too much to let it continue.

1. *To call for law enforcement.* The principal objective of C.D.L.'s picketing is to forcibly bring to the attention of the local authorities that the citizenry is demanding enforcement of the laws which govern the distribution and exhibition of obscene material. Picketing creates intense public pressure, calling for officials to enforce the laws against a crime that is being committed hourly, every day that those shops are open.

Fort Wayne had a laissez-faire attitude toward pornography. It just wasn't a priority item to the politicians or the law-enforcement officials. It wasn't a public issue. But persistent picketing changed all that.

2. *To demonstrate high community standards.* The secondary objective, closely allied, is to demonstrate in a visible fashion the contemporary standards in regard to tolerance, or intolerance, of obscene display within the community. The standards of the community are used by juries in their determination as to whether the material in question is obscene within the guidelines established by the United States Supreme Court.

A typical argument used by defense attorneys in

pornography cases runs like this: "Stores selling pornography already exist in the community. Therefore, the community standard tolerates pornography." It's circular logic, but it's typical. And unfortunately, some juries buy it. The power of picketing puts to rest that deceptive argument of the defense.

There's no way a jury can be persuaded that the community standard tolerates pornography when a broad base of five hundred of fifteen hundred or two thousand people from ten or twelve different denominations and civic organizations are signed up on a picketing roster, and walking the line seven days a week for two years. And that's precisely what happened in Fort Wayne, Indiana.

3. *To "out free-speech" the opposition.* Pornographers really don't know how to combat us when we picket. They often want to wrap themselves in the First Amendment protection (freedom of speech or of the press), and that's their chief line of defense. But picketing combines the First Amendment rights of citizens to "peaceably assemble for the redress of their grievances," and the right of free speech as expressed both by walking the picket line and by the signs the pickets carry. Putting people on the street who are exercising two First Amendment rights against pornographers' false claims to First Amendment rights puts the defense in a tight box, and they don't have a thing to say.

4. *To step across religious lines.* By asking for the enforcement of obscenity laws, rather than calling attention to religious principles, you encourage all the people of the community to join with you, and you prevent the media's dismissing you as religious fanatics. They will do so if given half a chance. Don't give them that. Picketing signs and public state-

ments must be restricted to calls for the local officials to do their duty in regard to the enforcement of the obscenity laws and clear statements of the community's commitment to decency. Signs with religious overtones must be avoided.

Picketing is only one facet of the community's overall strategy for eliminating the distribution and exhibition of obscene materials; it is not an end in itself.

The goal is not to humble someone or to appear to win. So far as possible, we want to have a win/win situation. If the 7-Eleven chain, for example, will take the porn out of its stores gracefully or make a show of "upholding family values" to its own advantage, fine. That makes a win/win situation, where our goals are achieved and the 7-Eleven people maintain respect.

Even as I emphasize the importance and propriety of picketing, I want to make the statement that not everybody needs to picket. People with physical restrictions should bow out. People who are experiencing trauma or emotional stress in their personal lives don't need additional burdens. There are people with the kind of temperament that makes public picketing extremely painful.

But perhaps most of us who feel reluctant to join the picket line really need to examine our hearts. This is the time to read about counting the cost of being a Christian (see Luke 14:25-35). Is our faith a comfortable habit or a costly life of discipleship? At what point do we put our lives on the line? The Psalmist says:

> Who rises up for me against the wicked?
>> Who stands up for me against evildoers?
> If the LORD had not been my help,

> my soul would soon have dwelt in the land of
> silence (Ps. 94:16-17).

Pornography puts the men, the women, and the children of our communities in danger of seduction, danger of rape, danger of abduction and murder. When people are in danger, it is time for action.

PREPARATION

Unfortunately, picketing is one of those things that can draw a certain type of person: rabble-rousers, zealots looking for a cause. You do *not* need these people on the picket line! When your team decides to picket, be absolutely sure that you start with the solid citizens and that you have very careful preparation.

Discipline is the underlying factor of successful teams:

(1) *Personal prayer and fasting*. Prayer is the first step, the last step, and every step along the way.

(2) *Thorough training on goals and strategy*. Each individual on the picket line must understand the basis for the action and the style in which to carry it out. The strategy must be crystal-clear so no one is confused or sidetracking effort into some vaguely related issue.

(3) *Maintain control at all times*. As Presbyterians, we often joke about our *Book of Order*, which admonishes us to do everything "decently and in order." In that sense, every picket line should be "Presbyterian." You are there to peaceably demonstrate, not to cause a confrontation.

In Fort Wayne, a team captain was in charge at each picketing site. Two-way radios provided instant communication between picketing teams at various locations and the team captains, who could readily contact the police at any sign of trouble. Keeping order is critical. Strict order also increases the credibility of the team; in two years of picketing in Fort Wayne, there were no serious incidents.

(4) *Only the team captain may talk to the media.* This is vitally important! Angry, belligerent talk destroys credibility and gives ammunition to the opposition. Be firm in instructing each member on the picket line, only the captain will speak to the media. Any individuals who will not cooperate in this spirit are not welcome to continue with the effort.

(5) *Effective community relations.* You will want the community to know that you have no desire to hurt other businesses, but rather to raise the tone of the local retail establishment. The neighboring businesses will stand behind your efforts if you approach them ahead of time with sensitivity for their concerns.

Make every effort to inform parents in the community of your goals and the reasons for your action. When parents realize the danger the distribution of pornography poses to their children, they will support you.

Talk to realtors and property owners. Sleazy porn outlets decrease property values in the area, so that realtors and investors lose money. You're working to their advantage, so ask for their active support.

(6) *Churches are the key to picketing.* In Fort Wayne, C.D.L. recruited pastors from all possible denominations, and the pastors recruited their flocks. When the picketing coordinator was setting up the monthly picketing schedule, he would call the church and say, "You're on every Wednesday this month, four to six P.M., in front of the Rialto Theater." Each church

was responsible for having people on the line for a specific, limited time, and they responded.

(7) *Utilize civic and social groups.* Call the PTA, the senior citizens' center, the YWCA and YMCA, and the local feminist group. The more diverse groups you have contributing visible support, the harder it will be for the opposition and media to dismiss you as representing "just the religious community."

(8) *Communicate with law enforcement officials ahead of time.* Ask for their recommendations on maintaining order and dealing with hecklers. Let them know that you're planning a long-term, peaceful demonstration, and you want to cooperate with them in every way.

Picketing isn't fun. People who come with the attitude that "this is going to be a good time," or that they're going to really "show those dirty so-and-so's," shouldn't be on the picket line at all.

Jesus said, "Blessed are those who mourn,...who hunger and thirst after righteousness" (Matt. 5:4-6). That's the Christian's motivation for picketing. Cultivate an attitude of compassion for the victims, hungering for righteousness, being willing to suffer ridicule, embarrassment, and persecution for the sake of the men and women who are being degraded and the children who are being destroyed.

"Blessed are you when men revile you and persecute you and utter all kinds of evil against you falsely on my account" (Matt. 5:11). Jesus knew what He was saying. He was reviled and mocked and spat on, for righteousness. Are you ready to follow His example?

Chuck Colson writes about Mother Teresa's visit to a troubled and neglected part of Washington, D.C., to start an outpost for her Sisters of Charity. The press was there in full force:

> "What do you hope to accomplish here?" someone shouted.
> "The joy of loving and being loved," she smiled, her eyes sparkling in the face of camera lights.
> "That takes a lot of money, doesn't it?"
> Mother Teresa shook her head. "No, it takes a lot of sacrifice."

A young mother, Susan Bell, who has given much time to the fight against pornography in Cincinnati, explained her reason for taking such a risk.

"I'd rather be home smocking dresses for my four girls—that's a dream I have of something I may be able to do once this problem is solved. Quite honestly, my involvement grew out of my concern to protect them. Many people say that I am bold, but I don't think I'm bold at all; I'm being obedient. To say to my Lord, 'No, God, I won't do it'—now *that* would be bold!"

ENDNOTES

1. For much of the material on boycotting we are indebted to Bishop Clyde E. Van Valin of the Free Methodist Church.

2. A study by Stanley Rothman and S. Robert Lichter in 1982 produced significant evidence of a wide disparity between the beliefs and values of those who control American media, the "TV elite," and the traditional beliefs and values of the general public.

Linda S. Lichter, S. Robert Lichter, and Stanley Rothman, "Hollywood and America: The Odd Couple," *Public Opinion*, Dec./Jan. 1983.

Stanley Rothman, and S. Robert Lichter, "Are Journalists a New Class?" *Business Forum*, Spring 1983.

3. For much of the material on picketing we are indebted to Thomas J. Blee, attorney in Fort Wayne, Indiana, member of the Board of Directors of Citizens for Decency Through Law, Inc., and the Executive Committee of Citizens for Decency Through Law of Fort Wayne, Indiana.

Chapter 11

Where the Battle Is Being Won

Let there be no pride or vanity in the work. The work is God's work....Put yourself completely under the influence of Jesus, so that he may think his thoughts in your mind, do his work through your hands, for you will be all-powerful with him who strengthens you.
Mother Teresa of Calcutta, quoted by Malcolm Muggeridge in
Something Beautiful for God, 48-49

Nothing happens to a man to bring him to change the world until he begins to challenge the way things are, dream of what could be, and put his life on the line to make it happen. In the words of George Bernard Shaw, "Some men look at what is and say, 'Why?' I look at what could be and say, 'Why not?' "
Larry Poland in *Rise To Conquer*, 31

The battle is being won in the hearts of people as never before.

Entire denominations are being mobilized. Local congregations are being informed and inspired to action. State organizations are emerging. Support for law enforcement and stronger legislation is growing. Victims and victimizers are having a change of heart and of lifestyle. All the national organizations are growing in number and strength. And they are working together.

Where the Battle Is Being Won

Local stores are removing pornographic magazines from their shelves. Whole chains of stores across the country are eliminating all pornographic materials. Don Wildmon of the National Federation for Decency has had a major role in encouraging such decisions and has provided this list of retail chains that have discontinued marketing "adult" magazines.

Make it a point to patronize:

Albertson's Food Stores
Bartell Drug Stores
Eckerd Drugs
Handy Mart Corporation
Handyway Stores
Kroger
King Kwik Food Stores
Marsh Supermarkets

Meijer Thrifty Acres
Pay 'n Save
Pen Supreme
  Grocerettes
Shop 'n Go
Skaggs Drug Stores
SuperX Drug Store
Tom Thumb
Wawa Convenience
  Stores

This is only a beginning, but it is a strong beginning. When you shop in any of these stores, express your appreciation of the moral principles that led to the decision to remove such material.

The battle is also being won on a citywide basis in metropolitan areas across the country because citizens are coming together to demand that the laws are enforced and that community standards are made known.

In the following accounts of the people who waged the battles, we've made a special attempt to realistically describe the struggle to overcome formidable, vicious opposition, without glossing over the difficulties.

THE FORT WAYNE STORY

Here are some further developments of the Fort Wayne story I've already introduced.

In April 1982, after five years of prayer alone and with others, Rev. Bob Yawberg met with six other men who had expressed deep concern over the growing violation of the Indiana law against obscenity. The adult bookstore was spoiling the tone of the whole neighborhood. Women became afraid to wait at the corner bus stop. Church members would find pages torn from magazines on the sidewalk where children had to walk to the Lutheran church's elementary school, less than a block away. Property values were falling and crime was rising.

Yawberg's team formed the seven-member executive committee of a local "Citizens for Decency through Law" (C.D.L.), adopting the name of the national nonprofit, nondenominational organization. They began by investing time in developing strong relationships with one another. Three goals were defined:

1. Daily prayer
2. Vigorous enforcement of existing laws
3. Strong community support

In June, a meeting was held with business and community leaders at the chamber of commerce. As the meeting began, a murmur of opposing voices grumbled about First Amendment rights and minding one's own business. But after the committee presented a ten-minute video sample of pornography and displayed magazines and other material available at the local outlets, the atmosphere changed. The community leaders who had previously been passive, had had no idea of the extent of perversion in their own town.

The participants at this meeting formed an eighty-two-member advisory board for the Fort Wayne C.D.L. They also signed cards allowing their names to appear in a half-page newspaper ad denouncing pornography.

C.D.L. members believed that support from the local churches would be crucial to the success of their efforts, so they invited all the area clergymen to breakfast meetings to present the problem and ask for support. They prayed for one hundred pastors to join the team. After two meetings, 118 ministers from forty-four denominations lined up with C.D.L. Eventually 172 religious leaders contributed active support. A meeting with Neighborhood Association Leaders saw fifty-two of them add their support. Together they developed the following action plan:

- They called for citizens of Fort Wayne to pray for the mayor, chief of police, prosecuting attorney, and workers for C.D.L. of Fort Wayne.
- They organized a strong base of community leaders from all segments of the city.
- They called for a meeting with the mayor. Forty-five advisory board members met in his office on July 14, 1982. In his statement to the media later that day, he instructed the city attorney to "begin a crackdown on all types of pornography."
- They called for the support of the chief of police and his men to carry out the mayor's order.
- They called for the prosecutor to prosecute and enforce existing Indiana laws against obscenity.

- They called for picketing as a demonstration of public support of prosecutions.

From the beginning, the elders of Broadway Christian Church knew that someone was going to have to push the action if it was going to have any chance of success. So they released Rev. Bob Yawberg from many of his normal pastoral duties, to devote at least half of his time to the antipornography campaign. The elders themselves and the laypersons took the burden of the ministry of the church.

Picketing began on August 10, 1982, with excitement, fear, and uncertainty as to what the public response would be. C.D.L. issued a carefully phrased statement to the media, making clear that it was asking only for enforcement of existing law.

An eighty-two-year-old grandmother marched regularly on the picket line. One of the porn "stars" came out of the theater and marched beside this lady, mocking and trying to intimidate her. Other porn supporters drove by, cursing the demonstrators and shouting obscenities. They spit at them, "mooned" them from car windows, threw tomatoes, and spattered them with water from toilets. Through all the harassment, the picketers remained silent and disciplined, so that in two years of picketing there were no violent incidents.

The porn operators claimed that the picketing had no effect on their business, yet went to great lengths to retaliate against C.D.L. At first they thought only Broadway Christian Church was doing the picketing, so they vented their anger against that congregation. One Sunday morning the manager of the porno store showed up at church. He was treated graciously like any other visitor.

So he tried another method. Young people were re-cruited with free coffee and doughnuts to picket the Broadway Christian Church on Sunday morning. Children and adults had to cross picket lines to get into Sunday school and the sanctuary. Members of other congregations driving by saw the pickets and called Broadway Christian to say that they were pray-ing in support. The mayor called to lend his personal encouragement.

One man in the pornographers' picket line wore a nun's habit and carried a sign, "What I read is *nun* of your business." Later, Roman Catholic Bishop Wil-liam McManus led the Catholic community in sup-port of the C.D.L. movement.

As the retaliation continued, members of the execu-tive committee were forced to take unlisted phone numbers because of harassing phone calls. Porn peo-ple stole the C.D.L. mailing list and sent out vicious countermailings. They took women's names from the list and put their names and phone numbers on the porn shops' marquees. Several C.D.L. leaders re-ceived bomb threats.

But as you might guess, the opposition backfired against the pornographers. It brought the commu-nity together in a firm commitment to wipe out por-nography in Fort Wayne.

Police gave continual protection to the C.D.L. pick-eters. One area company donated the use of two-way radios, so the captains of each picketing team were in constant communication with the others, with imme-diate access to police if trouble erupted.

Early on, it became apparent that the county prose-cutor was not making any realistic effort to enforce the law. At election time another candidate, Steve

Sims, took a strong stand on the issue, and the community voted him into office. Sims said it would take at least a year, but if C.D.L. would continue picketing, he would clean up the city.

Prosecutor Sims put action behind his campaign promises. Between July 1982 and August 1983, he obtained thirty-two convictions. These included trials by jury, convicting clerks for selling obscene merchandise. The jury was establishing and defining community standards.

Then the pornographers brought a six-hundred-thousand-dollar lawsuit against the police chief, the mayor, and C.D.L., stating that they had "incurred heavy legal fees, resulting from arrests, which threaten to bankrupt their business, and a substantial loss of income directly attributable to picketing."

After filing of the legal action, the three corporations and four of the seven individual plaintiffs were found guilty of distributing obscene material. The local jury resented their condescending manner and ruled against them. After multiple defeats in court, the pornographers dropped the lawsuit against C.D.L. and others.

In November 1982, Fort Wayne celebrated "Decency Week," a demonstration of religious unity. Over a thousand supporters marched and gathered to hear prayers and speeches, and to make a positive expression of their concern.

One year later, C.D.L. thought that November 1983 was going to be the point of victory. But the picketing had to continue through another northern Indiana winter. In all, two thousand volunteers had picketed over twenty-one thousand hours since August 10, 1982.

Then on March 19, 1984, prosecutor Sims called city and county police and outlined his plan. He obtained a court hearing on a R.I.C.O. (racketeering) charge. The judge issued an order of confiscation, and the police simultaneously hit and padlocked all three bookstores and confiscated all property, inventory, and bank accounts. Under Indiana civil R.I.C.O. statutes, all assets of the corporations became the property of the state, and the porn operators were effectively out of business. These cases are still on appeal, and prosecutor Sims is prepared to carry the fight to the Indiana Supreme Court, should it become necessary.

Still the picketing continued through the spring and summer at the one remaining porn outlet. Then on September 4, the South 27 Theater was closed, and the owner pleaded guilty to three counts of obscenity.

The president of the Fort Wayne historical society has requested the picketers' signs, all of the C.D.L. correspondence, and the videotapes, explaining that in future years, people will look back at this campaign as the turning point in Fort Wayne's moral climate.

THE CINCINNATI STORY

Back in 1967, Charles H. Keating began the fight against pornography in Cincinnati by successfully prosecuting three civil public nuisance abatement lawsuits against the movie "Vixen," Cinema X Theater, and "Oh! Calcutta!" Simon L. Leis, Jr., of Cincinnati was the first prosecutor in the country to completely rid a major city of all hard-core pornography, bookstores, and theaters. Apart from their efforts and those of Arthur Ney, who followed Simon Leis as prosecutor, and vice-squad leader Lt. Harold Mills what we are doing now in Cincinnati could never have been accomplished.

The recent developments in the Cincinnati story began with a sermon. On April 18, 1982, I opened my heart to our congregation and shared how I had seen broken lives and broken families among our own people, growing from the increasing tolerance of sexual immorality. I called the congregation to join me in six weeks of intense prayer.

From that Sunday until Pentecost, May 30, our congregation prayed and a small group of individuals, including graduate students, housewives, business leaders, and retired people, met each weekday morning at 6:30 to pray for God's guidance and help. We studied several books, including *The Death of Innocence* by Sam Janus; but mostly, we prayed. That led to the decision to meet weekly at 6:30 A.M. on Tuesdays for prayer and study until we knew the direction we ought to go.

In June, I went with several members of our church staff to view an "R" movie. It was a blatantly immoral film that mocked traditional values as prudery and made virtue out of promiscuity. Yet it was nothing out of the ordinary for contemporary films. I was ready to fight, but the congregation as a whole wasn't concerned.

"What are you making a fuss about? You're going to get laughed at for old-fashioned ideas," some told me. Good friends would take my arm and say, "Come on, Jerry, movies and magazines aren't that bad. Besides, you're fighting against the First Amendment." We had to find some way to bring understanding.

On July 28 we held an open meeting on moral concerns for our congregation, with presentations by the Honorable David Grossmann, Judge of Juvenile Court in Cincinnati; Dr. Gary Sweeten, the psychologist on our staff at College Hill Presbyterian Church; and other lay leaders from the prayer group. After the general meeting, we invited participants to view some film segments in a closed-door session. As expected, many who had been critical of our growing involvement had never actually seen pornography. Once they saw the film clips, the comments changed: "I had no idea...This is sickening...What can I do to stop this?"

As more of our own congregation and other churches in the community realized the extent of the problem, more joined us to study and pray. The team felt pulled in two directions with an urgent need to take strong action and an equally urgent need to take time to become knowledgeable and well equipped. We also realized that if we were going to mobilize churches effectively throughout the city, we'd need to have the commitment of the clergy.

On November 23 we hosted a breakfast for pastors across the city. These pastors continued to meet on the first Thursday of each month, while the local citizens' group at College Hill Presbyterian Church spawned other groups at churches in different parts of Cincinnati. In February and March I taught a class for laypersons, "A Time to Understand and to Stand," using John Court's book *Pornography: a Christian Critique*, as our text. Other classes followed, taught by those first students. Step by step, our base in the grassroots was growing, and our leadership was being strengthened.

In April 1983, Warner Amex Cable Company announced that the *Playboy* Channel was coming to Cincinnati on May 1. We unanimously decided that this was the time to take a public stand. It was at this time that we chose our name, Citizens Concerned for Community Values, and began to surface as an organized group.

C.C.C.V. began meeting with Cincinnati City Council members to protest the *Playboy* Channel. Several council members, particularly Ken Blackwell, agreed that Warner Amex had violated its contract with the city and especially its private correspondence during the negotiations, which expressly stated that the cable company would not bring in sexually explicit programming. But other council members disagreed and believed that Warner Amex had not broken the contract. They believed that any challenge to the contract should come from individual citizens.

Community stockholders, notably the Cincinnati Catholic Diocese and Xavier University, returned their shares to Warner Amex, because of their opposition to the *Playboy* Channel and their unwillingness to participate in obscenity. The Cincinnati Board of Education submitted a formal protest, urging city council to act against the cable company.

On May 20, we filled the chambers with over four hundred citizens to ask city council to test in the courts whether the original contract that the council had made with Warner Amex had been violated. We were preparing to pursue the issue, when suddenly Warner Amex made an out-of-court settlement with our county prosecutor, Arthur Ney, not to televise any X-rated or unrated films. It was also announced that the *Playboy* Channel could no longer be offered in Cincinnati because of "technical difficulties." Praise God for "technical difficulties"!

In the last months of 1983 and beginning of 1984, with the help of Juvenile Court Judge David Grossmann, attorney Tom Grossmann, and Councilman Ken Blackwell, C.C.C.V. was able to have a "display law" passed in Hamilton County requiring "adult" magazines to have shields concealing three-quarters of the magazines' covers. Our goal had been to require the magazines to be sold from under the counter as well, but that part of the ordinance was not passed.

Then on November 17-19, 1983, we sponsored the National Consultation on Pornography at the Marriott Inn in Cincinnati, hoping to raise national awareness and to stress the need for a coordinated effort against pornography nationwide.

THE NATIONAL CONSULTATION AND NATIONAL COALITION

In August of 1983, Donald Wildmon of the National Federation for Decency invited Christian leaders together in Tupelo, Mississippi, to consider a national strategy against pornography. At that time, he asked me to consider bringing the leaders of denominations together to join in the battle against pornography and obscenity nationwide. I immediately declined with regret: "God needs to use someone else."

But some days later, as I sat by a lake in Indiana where I had retreated for a time of prayer and planning, the vision of bringing leaders of antipornography groups and leaders of denominations together became a reality in my heart and mind.

The Mind Polluters

That, coupled with Don Wildmon's request, drove me to make phone calls to several of the national leaders against pornography: Brad Curl, Father Morton Hill, Bill Kelly, Bruce Taylor, and Don Wildmon. All five were available on November 18-20, the only days in the fall that we could have the Marriott Inn for a conference, free of charge. The National Consultation on Pornography was born.

Letters went out to denominational leaders, followed by numerous phone calls. Twenty-four denominational leaders representing eleven different denominations participated. At the closing luncheon, Bruce Taylor of C.D.L. surprised us by announcing his conviction that the National Consultation should continue as an entity and that I should serve as its chairman.

Each person I asked to serve on the cabinet accepted: Dr. R. Miltiades Efthemiou of the Greek Orthodox Church; Dr. Paul Tanner of the Church of God, Anderson, Indiana; Bishop Clyde E. Van Valin of the Free Methodist Church; and Dr. Jack H. White of Geneva College. We met together and by conference call, and decided a National Leadership Team should be formed, including the five of us, our five expert speakers, and five members of the C.C.C.V. steering committee. Every person who was asked to serve, agreed to serve.

In the two days of our organizational meeting, we agreed on our mission statement: "To mobilize the Christian community and all other concerned persons to combat and eliminate the destructive influence of obscenity, pornography, and indecency."

The Second National Consultation in 1984 brought together 360 leaders representing the three branches of the Christian church: Orthodox, Roman Catholic, and Protestant, including seventy-five denominations. We believe our role is first of all, to inform; second, to teach and model; third, to coordinate as many antipornography agencies as possible by mutual agreement; and finally, to assist and cooperate with local and national efforts so as to have the greatest possible impact against the presence of pornography.

We thank God for what He is doing, and for allowing us to be a part of His work.

THE COLUMBIA STORY

Two laymen, Steve Wooten and Richard McLawhorn, left the second National Consultation on Pornography with a message that was to change Columbia, South Carolina.

Representatives from twenty-five area churches were invited to hear Wooten and McLawhorn's report at Lexington Baptist Church. Plans to begin a local organization were announced, and some 120 people signed a list as those willing to be a part of a new movement against pornography.

A committee of about twelve persons began meeting regularly for prayer and discussion as to how to approach the problem. These became the steering committee, with Rev. Lewis Abbott as chairman, and adopted the name C.A.D.R.E.: Citizens Advocating Decency and a Revival of Ethics. Through the weeks and months, they struggled to put together a program that would stand up to the long haul. They developed a statement of purpose and a mission statement, became incorporated as a nonprofit organization, and obtained liability insurance for one million dollars to include legal fees if any suits are brought against them.

Lewis Abbott says, "The absolute necessity of having a 'God-called' steering committee can't be overstated. The entire effort is bathed in prayer and the authority of the Lord Jesus Christ has been acknowledged throughout the entire struggle."

Steering committee members were carefully and prayerfully chosen. Each person, including the chairman, had to be willing to be responsible for an action committee, and to be accountable for that work and for the attitude and approach of that committee. "Servant-heart" leadership is required of each member on this steering committee, and some individuals who were not willing to operate on that agenda were dropped.

Another source of C.A.D.R.E.'s remarkable success is its board of advisors. In order to reach the power establishment of the community—leading citizens and government leaders, religious as well as business leaders—the steering committee drew up a list of nominations. For three weeks the names on the list were discussed; some added, others eliminated. Finally, thirty individuals were approached by the steering committee. Through this process, the Lord raised up strong people with deep interest and concern in the problem of pornography, who also represent the leadership of the community.

Clear communication lines have been developed between steering committee members and advisory board members through mailings, personal letters, and frequent phone calls seeking advice. Each advisory board member has been made to feel that he or she is an important part of the organization's decision-making process. The advisory board is C.A.D.R.E.'s link to the power establishment in the community and is able to communicate effectively and open doors to any part of the community that is necessary.

In order to get membership growing in local organizations, the ingenious idea of the "C.A.D.R.E. Keys" was developed. A Key is a C.A.D.R.E. member who is also in a local organization such as a garden club, P.T.A., or medical society. The Key must be thoroughly educated on the problem of pornography, totally committed to the local and national effort, and willing to be a link with the C.A.D.R.E. office. That Key is responsible for membership enlistment and for giving broad educational information to his or her organization or group.

C.A.D.R.E.'s approach to the media is creative, rather than confrontational. In meeting with editors of the two large local newspapers, C.A.D.R.E. members ask for their advice as to how they would suggest the group should go about the effort against pornography. With this approach, C.A.D.R.E. is able to take a servant-heart attitude toward the press and, at the same time, obtain media support rather than opposition.

Finally, C.A.D.R.E. has learned to listen. Ideas that were contributed at the steering committee meetings are recorded and taken home by members and prayerfully considered before decisions are made. Leaders from other common-cause groups like battered women, abused children, and crisis rape centers, are invited to speak to the steering committee and share their work, expertise, and advice. Legal counsel at every step of the way has proved invaluable.

There is little doubt that Columbia, South Carolina, will be rid of pornography, obscenity, and indecency quickly and thoroughly, through the action of God and the obedience of dedicated people. What C.A.D.R.E. has accomplished in a few months can stand as a model of what is possible in every community in the United States.

ALLIES AT THE FRONT

I wish it were possible to describe in detail the achievements of other communities that have achieved major victories against pornography.

In Pittsburgh, Pennsylvania, the Pittsburgh Leadership Foundation, with the leadership of Reid Carpenter, has raised up grassroots support of community groups following the model of The Chemical People Project. Their Pittsburgh Coalition Against Pornography (P.C.A.P.) planted seeds in 1982 that encouraged the birth of Cincinnati's C.C.C.V. In 1983 P.C.A.P. held a workshop for district attorneys throughout the state to educate law-enforcement officials in how to effectively enforce Pennsylvania's anti-obscenity laws. By 1984, P.C.A.P. had a mailing list of forty-five hundred people and had made a significant contribution to the development of the National Coalition Against Pornography.

Then there is Atlanta, an example of what can be accomplished through good legislation and determined prosecutors. In 1975, the Georgia legislature rewrote the Criminal Code of Georgia to comply with the definition of obscenity given by the U.S. Supreme Court (*Miller*), and to provide that "any device designed or marketed as useful primarily for the stimulation of human genital organs" was obscene. That provision was particularly important.

The Supreme Court of Georgia ruled that the definition of obscene material does not apply to sexual devices, and that no search warrant is necessary to seize such devices displayed for sale in plain view. This statute was applied vigorously in Fulton County under the leadership of County Solicitor General Hinson McAuliffe. Through the years, convictions were obtained in at least 95 percent of all prosecutions, and by 1981, the last "adult" theaters, bookstores, and peep shows were closed in Fulton County. In 1984, Atlanta took the initiative to prosecute the "Miss America" issue of *Penthouse* (usually considered too "slick" to come under obscenity definitions) and succeeded in obtaining a significant conviction against the smut distributors.

Anderson, Indiana, is a model of what can be done with prayer, hard work, and firm resolve. Paul Tanner, executive secretary of the Church of God, attended the First National Consultation on Pornography in Cincinnati in 1983. He returned to Anderson with fire in his bones. He invited six key pastors of the city to lunch to share his burden. These six gained support from the City Ministerial Assembly to sponsor an "Awareness Meeting" in the city hall chambers. Civic leaders were invited, as well as area pastors and religious leaders.

Exactly eleven months after that first awareness meeting, "Citizens Concerned for Community Values" of Anderson is a thriving organization, mobilized for action with members representing seventeen different religious groups. The mayor, chief of police, and prosecuting attorney have addressed rallies held in City Hall Auditorium, and the local press and radio are giving enthusiastic support. Moreover, three "adult" bookstore owners have been arrested and are awaiting trial, and several local convenience stores have removed pornography from their shelves. Anderson is a city that is taking action.

Indianapolis is another important story. There the city and county council, with the support of Mayor William H. Hudnut, took courageous action in adopting a civil-rights ordinance in 1984, under which pornography is defined as a civil-rights violation and a form of sex discrimination. Because of suits joined by numerous pro-porn businesses, the Federal Court blocked the ordinances taking effect. But Mayor Hudnut and Indianapolis City Attorney John Ryan believe the ordinance is landmark legislation and expect the appeals to be taken to the Federal Supreme Court.

Now, in 1985, the Los Angeles County Board of Supervisors is considering a similar proposal. Under this new measure, every Los Angeles woman would have the right to bring a civil action against anyone who produces, sells, exhibits, or distributes obscenity that "presents women as dehumanized." Whether the proposal is adopted in Los Angeles or not, the message is being heard across the nation: women are not going to tolerate abuse by porn any longer!

I believe with all my heart that the tide is turning. The people of this land have said, "Enough!" People are ready to stand up and be counted.

We have started well. May the Lord continue to give us power and wisdom to see this battle through to a victorious end.

Chapter 12

Something to Give

It is an axiom in psychiatry that a plurality of direct sexual outlets indicates the very opposite of what it is popularly assumed to indicate. Dividing the sexual interest into several objectives diminishes the total sexual gratification, and men whose need for love drives them to the risks and efforts necessary to maintain sexual relationships with more than one woman show a deficiency rather than an excess in their masculine capacities.
Dr. Karl Minnenger, *Love Against Hate*, 72-73

Playboys grow old wondering why they are playing more and enjoying it less. They are missing the glory of sex because they have forgotten the sacredness of the gift.
William S. Banowsky, *It's a Playboy World*, 90

Brad Curl, the founder of the National Christian Association, suggests that pornographers have launched such vehement attacks against God and the church because they found out that Christians have better sex than they do! How can sex be good without joy? How can sex be good without deep trust or life-long commitment? Hedonists have stripped away from sex permanent, caring relationships, romantic love, tenderness, and gentleness. They isolate sex from the home and family, from the conceiving of children, from the mystery of sacrificial love. What do they have left? Mere biology.

THE CHRISTIAN WAY OF SEX

Often, too often, the Christian view of sex has been thought to be some kind of prudery, a denial of the enjoyment and warmth of sexual pleasure. Often, the world sets up a caricature of Victorian pomposity and attacks that image, accusing Christians of trying to limit sex to a biological necessity reluctantly permitted only for procreation with as little enjoyment involved as possible. A cursory reading of Song of Solomon suggests that nothing could be further from the truth!

I admit that unbalanced teaching has influenced Christian thinking at times, both in the Protestant and Catholic traditions. But that was our error; it was not the truth as revealed in the Word of God.

The Scriptures teach a holistic understanding of sex as something marvelous, created by God. Sex was His idea to begin with! It is good. Adam knew Eve in the Garden of Eden; it was not good for man to be alone. Sex was the bond of their human love, not the cause of their fall or an evil they got involved with after leaving the garden, as some would have us imagine. Sex was created by God and we should offer Him our thanks for it. It is His means both for creating children, and as the means of pleasure and love—a recreation of the relationship between husband and wife.

Jesus spoke of His relationship with the church as that of the lover and his bride, and of the Second Coming as the consummation of that marriage. If sex was not of God, would He have given us that image? The truth is that there is nothing more pure, beautiful, or joyful than the sexual relationship of a man and woman totally in love and totally committed to one another.

One doesn't need a degree in zoology or anthropology to see that human sex is far different than reproduction among the animals. We have freedom of control and of choice, freedom to express our sexuality in taking a spouse, or freedom to express our sexuality in chastity.

Sex is also a ministry—husband to wife and wife to husband, loving, comforting, caring, the giving of oneself to the other. This is the Christian understanding of sex. Holistic sexuality is a cornerstone in the Christian home.

Children who grow up in a loving, affectionate home where the mother and father obviously respect and enjoy one another will learn to seek that kind of relationship in their own marriages. In a home where there is modesty as well as honesty and respect for one another's bodies, children will learn that there is a holy mystery to sex. Children see and absorb their parents' concern for each other, their pleasure at being home again after separate work days or their excitement when coming together after a business trip. They see their parents' sharing problems and sorrows together, and they learn the trust, security, and joy of the Christian home.

This is sex that has time to grow, to mature, to develop into a skill that is expressed and exercised by and for both partners. Based on a lifetime of commitment, God allows each partner to learn how to please the other, to meet each other's deepest needs and desires. This sacrament of human love is custom-designed for one partner and one partner only. It is personalized; one-of-a-kind; just for her; just for him.

There is no way the playboy can experience this kind of sex. Nor can the hedonist thrill to the joy of pleasing a spouse for a lifetime.

Thus, we must challenge one another not only to rise up against pornography, obscenity, and indecency but also to proclaim with confidence that our new life in Christ brings with it the lasting joy of a righteous, holistic, joyful, guilt-free, and growing sexuality!

HEALING THE BROKENHEARTED

For these reasons, we need to let the victims of the *Playboy* philosophy know there is hope in Jesus Christ. We need to tell them there is healing and help, forgiveness and acceptance in the community of believers. But as we proclaim that hope, we must be committed to *be* that healing community.

Recall Dr. Elizabeth Holland's words: "I can cure venereal disease. I can stitch up the lacerations and put ointment on the wounds. But I cannot touch the damage and the scars that have been inflicted on the minds, and hearts, and spirits." Dr. Nicholas Groth, psychologist at the Connecticut Correctional Institute, posits, "Abusers are never cured."

It is Jesus Christ who heals the victims and forgives and transforms the offenders. Jesus promised, "He has sent me to proclaim release to the captives/and recovering of sight to the blind,/to set at liberty those who are oppressed" (Luke 4:18). First John 1:9 says, "If we confess our sins, he is faithful and just, and will forgive our sins and cleanse us from all unrighteousness." *All* unrighteousness.

God can heal the spirit of a girl raped in childhood.

He can heal the memories of the woman beaten and misused by her husband. I have prayed and counseled with many of the victims, and I have seen them wonderfully healed and restored to wholeness through Jesus Christ.

God can forgive and heal the porn model. God can forgive and heal the child molester. God can forgive and heal the homosexual. There is no sin too great for God to forgive, no wound too deep for Him to heal. And He will do it through us.

In the eighteenth century, immorality was ravaging England, until the Wesleyan revival turned that nation upside down. But Christians had to face up to their own unrighteousness within the body of Christ itself before they could change their national unrighteousness.

There can be no toleration of immorality, factionalism, or petty disputes among ourselves. We must be satisfied with nothing less than the total lordship of Jesus Christ. Only then can the church be the therapeutic community to those who are broken. The church must learn to be the community of healing that is willing and able to let the power of God's love flow through us to the brokenhearted of our society.

ARDOR WITH ORDER

"Be angry but do not sin" (Eph. 4:26). It is right to be angry about the sins of pornography and immorality. We must have righteous—healing—anger against sin. Our anger must never be directed at people or things, but at the devil and his activities.

We must never forget that righteous anger against sin burns in the heart of God because of His great desire to save the lost. "But I say to you, love your enemies and pray for those who persecute you, so that you may be sons of your Father who is in heaven" (Matt. 5:44). If our anger is misdirected and drives the pornographer or the porn addict farther from God, then we have unwittingly become agents of evil, not of God.

Peter Gillquist, presiding bishop of the Evangelical Orthodox Church, has taught me to pray this simple prayer of humility for an offender: "Lord, do not let him perish through me, a sinner." It is a priestly prayer of one who is attempting to bring an enemy of God to repentance.

God hates the sin, but He loves the sinner. God intends to love the sinner through His people, the church. Are we willing to let Him love the sinner through us? Are we willing to mourn for sin, to hunger and thirst after righteousness? Are you willing to lay down your life to stop the flood of pornography in our nation?

A little town in the west was traumatized by a little three-year-old girl's disappearance. The parents became frantic and sought help from the police. Three days and nights of searching produced no clues. The community gathered together to pray and to seek to take further action.

Then a young man spoke up. "I've been thinking about that big field south of town. It's over a mile wide and a couple of miles long. The grass is nearly three feet tall. Maybe she's there. If we all gathered at one end and took hands, we could stretch all the way across the field and walk the whole length of it together. Are you with me?"

A glimmer of hope led them out to the field. They

took hands and began to walk. About two-thirds of the way, a shout went up. "She's here! She's here!"

And then a scream of agony. "She's dead! O, God, she's dead!"

As they carried the little girl's body back into town in the midst of tears, someone was heard to say, "If we had only gotten together and taken hands sooner, she would have been alive."

If we had gotten together sooner for the battle against pornography, thousands of children would still be alive, millions of women would not have been raped, an entire generation of young people would not have been ravaged through drugs and twisted death-dealing sex.

Let's take hands and walk together. We have the people necessary. We have the financial resources required to do the job. But we have not had the commitment. Pastors, laypersons, let's take hands and unite the entire Christian community across the nation and within each community, to say no to the kingdom of darkness.

I beg of you to take these things that you have learned, these weapons for good in the war against impurity, and use them to preserve the lives and dignity of those who are your companions on the earth. And may the power of the Father, Son, and Holy Spirit be yours to do battle and to win.

Make this your prayer:

Lord! I 'll be whatever you want me to be;
I 'll do whatever you want me to do;
I 'll go wherever you want me to go;
I 'll say whatever you want me to say;
And I 'll give away whatever you want me to give away.

Appendix I

Operational Statement For
National Coalition Against Pornography

I. *Mission Statement*

To mobilize the Christian community and all concerned citizens to combat and eliminate the destructive influences of obscenity, pornography, and indecency.

II. *Role*

1. Inform, mobilize, and assist denominational, religious network, and other leaders in carrying out the stated mission, while recognizing and respecting the autonomy of each group.
2. Teach and model a leadership style incorporating mutual love, trust, individual worth, and decision by consensus in dependence on the Holy Spirit.
3. Coordinate with agencies of similar purpose such as Morality in Media, Inc.; Citizens for Decency Through Law, Inc.; National Federation for Decency; and the National Christian Association.
4. By mutual agreement, assist and cooperate with religious, civic, citizens, and other groups involved in the effort to eliminate the destructive in-

The Mind Polluters

fluences of obscenity, pornography, and indecency.

III. *Objectives*
1. Area I—"Christian View of Persons." Objective: Lift the moral standards in America to a level that supports family life in keeping with Judeo-Christian values and applies God's justice to the human dilemma by providing respect for the personhood of each man, woman, and child, in every ethnic group.
2. Area II—"Involvement." Objective: Develop a strategy with denominational, religious network, and parachurch leaders which will combat and eliminate the destructive influences of obscenity, pornography, and indecency. We will seek agreement on a priority issue each year.
3. Area III—"Moral Values in Media." Objective: Assist the Christian community and concerned citizens in demanding from the media the highest standards of traditional morality and decency.
4. Area IV—"Adult Bookstores, Obscene Movies and Videos." Objective: Seek to eliminate operation of all enterprises that debase individuals by catering to that which is obscene, pornographic, or indecent.
5. Area V—"Law Enforcement." Objective: Demand from the president and all proper authorities the enforcement of all obscenity, pornography, and indecency laws. Encourage new laws at all levels of government where necessary to eliminate destructive influences of obscenity, pornography, and indecency.
6. Area IV—"Child Sexual Exploitation and Abuse." Objective: Protect and deliver children who are victims of sexual exploitation and abuse.

Appendix II

RESOLUTION ON PORNOGRAPHY AND OBSCENITY

WHEREAS, in the last few years there has been an explosive escalation of the portrayal of sexual immorality and deviation, profanity, alcoholism, and other drug abuse, and demonic violence on television and radio; and,

WHEREAS, the lifestyle which is modeled for our children on the mass media outlets which portray these excesses without regard for time of day or age of audience is potentially dehumanizing and morally destructive; and,

WHEREAS, many of the ideals lifted up on mass media programming are in direct contradiction to those lifestyle ideals which are proclaimed and modeled in the gospel of Jesus Christ; and,

WHEREAS, we are called as members of the church of Jesus Christ to allegiance to those ideals; and,

WHEREAS, the General Assemblies of both the former U.P.C.U.S.A. and the P.C.U.S. have acted in response to violence, sexual exploitation for commercial purposes, and lax morality in the public media; and,

WHEREAS, the former P.C.U.S. at its one hundred twenty-first General Assembly (1981) recorded its opposition to themes of violence and immorality in the public media, and further called for appropriate federal agencies to employ their influence to eliminate extreme portrayals of these themes in the public media; and,

WHEREAS, the former U.P.C.U.S.A. at the one hundred eighty-ninth General Assembly (1977) adopted a resolution, "to take a public stand against the use of pornography and violence in the media and to reinforce the dignity of human beings, and thereby strengthen the Christian faith"; and,

WHEREAS, among the comments which have been made by past General Assemblies, the one hundred eighty-

The Mind Polluters

fifth General Assembly (1973) noted a concern for the following problem areas as they are portrayed in the mass media:

a. glorification of violence and its numbing effect on ethical standards;

b. commercialization and exploitation of sex;

c. overt appeals to materialism as the ideal style of life;

d. emphasis on advertising instant relief of problems through medication; and,

WHEREAS, pastors, counselors, social agencies, and law officials are seeing families broken and lives adversely affected, as well as persons of both sexes and of all ages victimized by pornography and obscenity; and,

WHEREAS, pornography, "kiddie porn," and materials depicting excessive violence and murder combined with sexual content are part of a growing six-billion-dollar industry (more than the movie and record industry combined) controlled largely by organized crime (ranked as their third largest money-maker); and,

WHEREAS, the Supreme Court of the United States in 1973 established basic guidelines for determining "what is obscene"; and,

WHEREAS, the Supreme Court of the United States has traditionally held that obscenity is not protected by the First Amendment and that obscenity is not protected expression; and,

WHEREAS, there are existing federal and state laws to stem the rampant flow of obscene materials and to control their availability; therefore, be it

RESOLVED. That the one hundred ninety-sixth General Assembly (1984) of the Presbyterian Church (U.S.A.) to:

1. direct the Stated Clerk to notify the President of the United States that it is the desire of the General Assembly of the Presbyterian Church (U.S.A.) to have the laws related to obscenity enforced by the U.S. Attorney General

and the U.S. Attorneys, the U.S. Postal Service, the Commerce Department, and the Customs Department. And that the PC (U.S.A.) is supportive of current efforts to include obscenity under the R.I.C.O. Statutes; (R.I.C.O. Statutes: Racketeering-Influenced and Corrupt Organizations statutes currently cover obscenity. Legislation to this effect was introduced into the House and Senate on 11-14-83).

2.   mandate the Council on Women and the Church and the General Assembly Mission Board (Office of Women) to persevere in their work in the areas of pornography and obscenity and the education of the church and society to combat the abusive treatment of women;

3.   establish official, visible relationship with other denominations and their leaders who are taking action against obscenity and pornography;

4.   encourage every Presbyterian to:

   a.   develop awareness of the depth of the problem and its implications for the church and the world;

   b.   take an active supportive role in one of the organizations working to establish the enforcement of current laws;

   c.   refrain from supporting economically all motion pictures offensive to that individual's personal and moral convictions, and refrain from supporting economically companies that sponsor TV or radio programs or advertise in media in ways offensive to that individual's personal moral convictions;

   d.   file objections with the management or refuse to patronize those businesses which they personally feel contribute to the moral decay of our homes and families;

   e.   write personally to those against whom the above action has been taken, informing them of the action and the reason for it; and,

The Mind Polluters

5. call on our churches to minister to both those who have become victimizers, and those who are or who have been victimized by violence, pornography, and sexual abuse, affirming the love of God and the new life in Jesus Christ that is for all persons.

Adopted by the General Assembly of the Presbyterian Church (U.S.A.), June 1984.

A NAZARENE COMMITMENT

Delegates gathered in this _____ annual Assembly of the _____ District Church of the Nazarene make this statement of concern, confession, and commitment.

We have CONCERN for this social and moral atmosphere of our communities and cities...

CONCERN that the laws have become so permissive and tolerance so complete that the will to protect our communities and children from moral filth may be dissolved;

CONCERN that the new technical tools of broadcast, video, films, photography, and printing, lacking in other generations, have come under control of perverted minds to be used by greedy people without regard for the moral well-being of this civilization;

CONCERN that pornography involving children, sex with animals, and every other perversion is now backed by big money, the organized underworld, and certain mass media whose self-serving appeal to "rights" and "freedom" is only a cover to practice the distribution of their filth from coast to coast to corrupt and to subvert, until centers of pornography become centers of vice.

We humbly CONFESS as members of the body of Christ that we have not been faithful witnesses in facing the moral decline in our society...

We CONFESS that unconsciously we have allowed the

212

national entertainment media (55 percent of whom say they have no religion and 93 percent of whom acknowledge they seldom or never attend worship) set our moral standards and dictate the tone of family living by turning our homes into nonstop TV studios;

We CONFESS, like the early Methodist class meeting, that "we have failed to rebuke men for their sins" and have faltered in prophetically proclaiming God's judgment upon the floodtide of obscenity, perversion, and violence which saturates so much of modern movies, advertising, publications, radio, and television. We have carelessly absorbed from the media pitchmen selling us the notions that adulterous living is normal, and even desirable; that homosexual practices comprise an acceptable alternate lifestyle; and that drugs, alcohol, and violence have honored places in life—all of which flaunt biblical commands.

We are COMMITTED to Jesus Christ, the Lord of the church, who calls us to be the "salt of the earth" and the "light of the world...."

We, therefore, COMMIT ourselves to be the most effective witnesses possible, as God gives us talent and influence, against the violence, vulgarity, profanity, and anti-Christian programming on television;

We COMMIT ourselves to worthily challenge the hedonism, materialism, and humanism that will leave our society devoid of the Christian view of man and without the base for determining law and justice or right and wrong, if we fail;

We COMMIT ourselves to cooperation with other churches and organizations locally to support community decency standards and to encourage judges, juries, and other law enforcement officials in their responsibilities to protect the community from the exploitation of pornography in films, video, magazines, and lewd businesses;

We COMMIT ourselves to united ACTION STEPS THAT CAN MAKE A DIFFERENCE:

The Mind Polluters

1. We can Pray
2. We can Read
3. We can Study
4. We can Survey
5. We can Speak
6. We can Write
7. We can Organize
8. We can Get Professional Help
9. We can Set an Example
10. We can Adopt Projects

We COMMIT our way unto the Lord, with full assurance that evildoers and workers of iniquity "shall soon be cut down like grass and wither as a green herb....And He shall bring it to pass....For evildoers shall be cut off: but those that wait upon the Lord, they shall inherit the earth" (Ps. 37:1, 2, 5, 9).

A NAZARENE STATEMENT

A Response to the Effect of the Playboy Mentality on Our Society.

We are Nazarenes who are concerned about the effects of all forms of pornography upon our community. As an international group of Christians, we have witnessed the pursuit of hedonism and selfish materialism—the playboy mentality—become the lifestyle in much of the Western world and especially in the United States of America. We have watched while young children have been enslaved and sold as sexual merchandise to fuel the pornographic industry. We are appalled that the entertainment media with its emphasis on casual promiscuity has become a major tool for degradation of true human sexuality.

We have observed the personnel within the pornography industry become honored celebrities. We see the commerce of our land support this destructive trend by pouring millions of dollars into the advertising coffers of the pornographic industry. Most importantly, too often we see the responsible Christian men and women in our society condone this philosophy by their silence.

We call upon Nazarenes in every society and community

to stand in opposition to this rapidly growing pornography industry and its increasing effect upon our communities, especially the young families and the youth. No nation can afford a lifestyle which annually produces one million unwed pregnant teen-agers, untold numbers of abortions, massive psychological damage, and rampant rates of divorce and venereal disease. Nazarenes must not keep silent about this playboy mentality, a philosophy that has no room for the aged, the sick, the poor, or the unlovely.

We call on our members everywhere to appeal to their business communities to cease the sales and circulation of pornography. We call upon all businesses to discontinue advertising in any form of media which encourages the growth of this playboy mentality and the destruction of our families and homes.

As Christians, we recognize that this situation often exists because we have been silent. We commit ourselves to the reaffirmation of scriptural principles which promote human dignity, protect our children from sexual exploitation, and provide healthy roles for the expression of human sexuality.

General Christian Action Committee
Church of the Nazarene

Appendix III

Proposed Law for the State of Ohio and Other States

No person, with knowledge of its character, shall promote within the state of Ohio any visual portrayal of ultimate sexual acts, whether by printed material or filmed material, by airwaves or wireless communication, for purposes of commercial entertainment.

"Promote" includes manufacture, issue, sell, give, provide, advertise, produce, reproduce, lend, mail, import, cause to be sent or brought into this jurisdiction, deliver, transfer, transmit, publish, distribute, circulate, broadcast, disseminate, present, display, exhibit, pose for, perform, participate in, advertise, or to offer or agree, or possess with intent, to do any of the activities described above.

"Ultimate sexual acts" means intercourse, sodomy, cunnilingus, fellatio, analingus, and masturbation, where the penetration or ejaculation of human genital organs is visible.

Pictures involving sadomasochistic sexual activities or pictures of penis erection in scenes suggesting that penetration or oral sex were imminent are also proscribed.

This statute does not apply to ultimate sexual acts which are portrayed or employed for bona fide scientific, medical, educational, psychological, or law enforcement purposes. Nor does it apply to newspapers, books, magazines, or other printed matter unless they contain pictures of ultimate sexual acts as described in the statute for other than the purposes described above.

The proposed federal law would read:

It shall be illegal, with knowledge of its character, to import or to transport, mail or otherwise distribute through interstate commerce whether by printed material or filmed material, by airwaves or by wireless communication, any visual portrayal of ultimate sexual acts for purposes of commercial entertainment.

"Ultimate sexual acts" means (see above)
This statute does not apply to (see above)
Reo M. Christenson

Appendix IV

Model Cable Television Law

Section 1

(a) No person (including franchisee) shall by means of a cable television system, knowingly distribute by wire or cable to its subscribers any indecent material or knowingly provide such material for distribution.

(b) "Person" shall include individuals, partnerships, associations, and corporations.

(c) "Distribute" shall mean send, transmit, or retransmit or otherwise pass through a cable television system.

(d) "Material" means any visual material shown on a cable television system, whether or not accompanied by a soundtrack, or any sound recording played on a cable television system.

(e) "Indecent material" shall mean material which is a representation or verbal description of:
1. a human sexual or excretory organ or function; or
2. nudity; or
3. ultimate sexual acts, normal or perverted, actual or simulated; or
4. masturbation; which under contemporary community standards for cable television is patently offensive.

(f) "Community standards" shall mean the standards of the community encompassed within the territorial area covered by the franchise.

(g) "Provide" means to supply for use.

(h) "A person acts knowingly" if he has knowledge of the character or nature of the material involved. A person is presumed to have knowledge of the character or nature of the material if he has actual notice of the nature of such material whether or not he has precise notice of its contents.

Section 2

Violation of this statute shall constitute a misdemeanor and any person convicted of such violation shall be confined in jail for not more than _____ months or fined not more than _____ dollars, either or both.

Appendix V

Citizens for Decency through Law, Inc.—William Swindell,
National Director
2331 West Royal Palm Road
Phoenix, Arizona 85021

Morality in Media, Inc.—Rev. Morton A. Hill, S.J.,
475 Riverside Drive
New York, N. Y. 10115

National Christian Association—Brad Curl
P. O. Box 40945
Washington, D. C. 20016

National Coalition Against Pornography—Richard McLawhorn,
Executive Director
P. O. Box 24K
Cincinnati, Ohio 45224

National Federation for Decency—Rev. Donald E. Wildmon,
Executive Director
P. O. Drawer 2440
Tupelo, Mississippi 38803

BIBLIOGRAPHY

Anson, Sam and Cara Morris, "Why Men Rape," *Mademoiselle*, January 1982, 108-110.

Bandura, Albert. *Principles of Behavior Modification*. New York: Holt, Rinehart and Winston, 1969.

Banowsky, William S. *It's a Playboy World*. Old Tappen, N.J.: Revell, 1969.

Bullheimer, Paul E. *Destined for the Throne*. Minneapolis: Bethany House, 1975.

Burgess, Ann, A. Nicholas Groth, and M.S. McClousland. "Child Sex Initiation Rings," *American Journal of Orthopsychiatry*, 51:(1981), 110-19.

Chambers, Oswald. *My Utmost for His Highest*. New York: Dodd, Mead, 1935.

Cline, Victor B., *Where Do You Draw the Line?* Provo, Utah: Brigham Young University Press, 1974. "Aggression Against Women: the Facilitating Effects of Media Violence and Erotica." (Presented to the associated students of the University of Utah, Salt Lake City, April 3, 1983.)

Colson, Charles. *Loving God*. Grand Rapids: Zondervan, 1983.

Court, John H. *Pornography: A Christian Critique*. Downers Grove, Ill: Inter-Varsity Press, 1980.

Densen-Gerber, Judianne, and S. Hutchinson, "Medical-Legal and Societal Problems Involving Children," in *The Maltreatment of Children*, ed. Selwyn Smith. Baltimore: University Park, 1978.

Dworkin, Andrea. *Pornography*. New York: Putnam, 1981.

Fortune, Marie Marshall. *Sexual Violence...the Unmentionable Sin, An Ethical and Pastoral Perspective*. New York: Pilgrim, 1983.

Foster, Richard J. *Celebration of Discipline*. San Francisco: Harper and Row, 1978.

Gallagher, Neil. *The Porno Plague*. Minneapolis: Bethany House, 1981.

Gray, Susan H. "Exposure to Pornography and Aggression Toward Women: the Case of the Angry Male," *Social Problems*, 4 (1982), 387.

Groth, A. Nicholas. *Men Who Rape, The Psychology of the Offender*. New York: Plenum, 1979.

Guio, M., A. Burgess, and R. Kelly, "Child Victimization: Pornography & Prostitution," *Journal of Crime and Justice*, 3 (1980), 65-81.

The Hearing Concerning Sexually Explicit Publications. (Testimony before the Subcommittee on Juvenile Justice, Committee on the Judiciary, United States Senate, Washington, D.C., August 8, 1984.)

Heschel, Abraham. *The Prophets*, vol. 2. New York: Harper and Row, 1962.

Hill, Morton A., Winfrey C. Link, and Victor Cline, consultant. *The Hill-Link Minority Report of the Presidential Commission on Obscenity and Pornography*, 1970, Washington, D.C.

It's O.K. to Say No! coloring and activity books. New York: Creative Child Press, and Waldman Publishing Corp., 1984.

Janus, Sam. *The Death of Innocence*. New York: Morrow, 1981.

Johnson, Robert Clyde. *The Meaning of Christ*. Philadelphia: Westminster, 1958.

Keating, Charles. *Report to the President's Commission on Obscenity and Pornography*, 1970.

Kirk, Jerry. *The Homosexual Crisis in the Mainline Church*. Nashville, Tenn.: Thomas Nelson, 1978.

Laubach, Frank. *Prayer, the Mightiest Force in the World*. Westwood, N.J.: Revell, 1946.

Lederer, Laura, ed. *Take Back the Night*. New York: Morrow, 1980.

MacDonald, Hope. *Discovering How to Pray*. Grand Rapids: Zondervan, 1976.

Malamuth, N.M. and E. Donnersten. *Pornography and Sexual Aggression*. New York: Academic Press, 1984.

Marshall, Catherine. *Adventures in Prayer*. New York: Ballantine, 1980.

Martin, Lloyd and Jill Haddad. *We Have a Secret*. Newport Beach, Calif.: Crown Summit Books, 1982.

Muggeridge, Malcolm. *Something Beautiful for God: Mother Teresa of Calcutta*. Garden City, New York: Doubleday, 1977.

O'Brien, Shirley. *Child Pornography*. Dubuque, Iowa: Kendall/Hunt Publishing Company, 1983.

Poland, Larry. *Rise to Conquer: A Call of Committed Living*. Chappaqua, N. Y.: Christian Herald Books, 1979.

Rothman, Stanley and Robert S. Lichter. "Are Journalists a New Class?" *Business Forum*, Spring 1983.

Schlesinger, L., ed. *Sexual Dynamics of Anti-Social Behavior*. Springfield, Ill.: Charles C. Thomas Publishers, 1983.

Scott, David, ed. *Symposium on Media Violence and Pornography, Proceeding Resource Book and Research Guide*. Toronto, Canada: Media Action Group, 1984.

ten Boom, Corrie. *Amazing Love*. Fort Washington, Pa.: Christian Literature Crusade, 1953.

To Establish Justice, to Insure Domestic Tranquility, The Report from the National Commission on the Causes and Prevention of Violence. New York: Award Books, 1969.

"The War Within: An Anatomy of Lust," *Leadership*, Fall 1982, 31-48.

Zillmann, Dolf and Jennings Bryant. "Pornography, Sexual Callousness, and the Trivialization of Rape," *Journal of Communication*, 4 (1982), 10.

Study materials, audio and videotapes of the first and second National Consultations on Obscenity, Pornography, and Indecency are available from:

The National Consultation on Pornography
5835 Hamilton Avenue
Cincinnati, Ohio 45223